LET ME GO

Helga Schneider was born in Steinberg, then in Germany, now in Poland, and spent her childhood in Berlin where, after being abandoned by her mother, she was raised by her stepmother. Since 1963 she has lived in Bologna.

ALSO BY HELGA SCHNEIDER

The Bonfire of Berlin

Helga Schneider

LET ME GO

TRANSLATED FROM THE ITALIAN BY
Shaun Whiteside

VINTAGE

Published by Vintage 2005

9

First published in Great Britain in 2004 by
William Heinemann

Translated from the Italian,
Lasciami andare madre

Vintage
Random House, 20 Vauxhall Bridge Road,
London SW1V 2SA

Random House Australia (Pty) Limited
20 Alfred Street, Milsons Point, Sydney
New South Wales 2061, Australia

Random House New Zealand Limited
18 Poland Road, Glenfield,
Auckland 10, New Zealand

Random House (Pty) Limited
Endulini, 5A Jubilee Road, Parktown 2193,
South Africa

The Random House Group Limited Reg. No. 954009
www.randomhouse.co.uk/vintage

A CIP catalogue record for this book
is available from the British Library

ISBN 978 0 099 44374 2

Penguin Random House is committed to a sustainable future for
our business, our readers and our planet. This book is made from
Forest Stewardship Council® certified paper.

Printed and bound in Great Britain by Clays Ltd, St Ives plc

'The feeling of hatred has always been alien to me.'

Rudolf Höss, commandant of the Auschwitz death camp

To Daniela

Vienna, Tuesday 6 October 1998,
in my hotel

Today, mother, I am going to see you for the first time in twenty-seven years, and I am wondering whether in all that time you have ever understood how much damage you did to your children. I didn't sleep a wink last night. It's almost daylight now; I've opened the shutters. A smoky veil of light is brightening above the roofs of Vienna.

I'm going to see you again today, mother, but what will I feel? What can a daughter feel for a mother who refused to be a mother, so that she could become a member of Heinrich Himmler's evil organisation?

Respect? Only for your age – nothing else. And apart from that?

It would be hard to say that I don't feel anything. You're my mother, after all. But I can't say it will be love. I can't love you, mother.

I'm in a state of agitation, and in spite of myself I'm thinking about our last meeting, in 1971, when I saw you again for the first time in thirty years, and I shudder to remember my dismay upon discovering that you had been a member of the SS.

And you hadn't even shown any remorse. You were

still perfectly content about your past, about what you had been, about that efficient factory of horrors where you had been a model worker.

It's seven o'clock, a pale sky; it's going to rain. And I'm going to see you today, mother, for the second time since you abandoned me, fifty-seven years ago: a lifetime. I'm becoming aware of a sense of bitter excitement, of impatience. Because in spite of everything, you're still my mother.

What will we say to each other? What will you say to me? Will I find any trace in you of regret for what we've never had? Will you have that motherly caress for me, the one I've spent more than half a century waiting for? Or will you torment me once more with your indifference?

In 1971 I was living in Italy and had a little son, Renzo; all of a sudden I felt an uncontrollable need to track you down. I found you. And I hurried to Vienna with my son to hug you again. But you treated that grandson of yours, that boy who looked at you with such keen curiosity, with frosty detachment, denying him the right to a grandmother, just as you had denied me my right, in the end, to have a mother. Because you didn't want to be a mother. Ever since we were born, you always entrusted me and my brother Peter to other people. And yet in the Third Reich, motherhood was obsessively praised, particularly by the Propaganda Minister, Josef Goebbels.

Even Heinrich Himmler, the Reichsführer of the SS, your boss, mother – maintained that there was one principle that his members must unfailingly obey: honesty, loyalty and fidelity towards people with the same blood as oneself. Did your children not share your blood?

4

No, you didn't want to be a mother; you preferred power. Faced with a group of Jewish prisoners you felt omnipotent. A guard in charge of famished, exhausted and desperate Jews, heads shaved, eyes vacant – what a despicable kind of power, mother!

I stare at Vienna's inhospitable sky, and find myself being filled with an impulse to rebel: I regret replying so diligently to the call of a stranger. I should have ignored it, I tell myself; I should have let things drift along as they have for the last thirty years.

I was too hasty in deciding to leave.

The letter had arrived one day in late August, and for some strange reason it had filled me with apprehension even before I opened it. What on earth could be inside that disgusting pink envelope? I wasn't expecting any post from Vienna. I had left the city in 1963, and from then on I had lost all contact with my old friends.

The writer of the letter was a woman called Gisela Freihorst, who said she had been a dear friend of my mother. That was how I learned that my mother was still alive.

Yes, she was still alive, but she had recently been transferred to a *Seniorenheim*, an old people's nursing home. Her condition was deteriorating: she would leave her house and get lost, she would forget to turn off the water, or, even worse, the gas, and risk blowing up the entire building. All in all, as they say in such cases, she had become a danger to herself and to other people.

At first she had been looked after by her local mental

health service: she had to attend the day hospital for the elderly three times a week, and the rest of the time she was visited by various kinds of social worker. She always sent them away with a flea in their ear; clearly the years had done nothing to sweeten her character, which had always been suspicious, confrontational and rebellious. But in the end the decision had been taken to remove her from her flat and place her in an environment where she could be monitored day and night.

'Your mother is approaching the age of ninety,' the letter concluded, 'and she could pass away from one day to the next. Why not consider the possibility of meeting her one last time? After all, she is still your mother.'

Those words, at once plain and bureaucratic, disturbed me profoundly. After my bruising encounter with my mother in 1971, I had buried her memory in a dark recess of my mind. For many years I was convinced that my virtual burial of her had somehow become real. I imagined my mother interred in one of those haunting cemeteries in Vienna, the city where both she and my father were born. That same Vienna where I had lived as a girl, at school, lonely and resentful; the city that I had admired but never loved. Vienna with its ancient imperial pride; rigorous, polite, green, clean, frosty Vienna.

That Vienna which even today from a distance of twenty-seven years, I still observe with a kind of suspicious fascination.

And I had been fooling myself all along. That letter in its disgusting pink envelope dragged me out of my cosy conviction that my mother was dead, and that I would never again have to confront torments and pain on her account.

It is twenty past seven, and it's starting to drizzle. The gloomy sky is aggravating my unease.

I should have ignored the letter, I'm becoming more and more convinced of it. I would have been unsettled for several days, and then I would gradually have buried it along with all the rest, slipping once more towards some semblance of tranquillity. And yet I didn't. I allowed myself to be overwhelmed by the news, by Frau Freihorst's sad words. Or perhaps it was just my own curiosity: what would my mother look like today?

Or was it rather a small and foolish hope that was awakening in me? Perhaps she would have changed; perhaps her great age would have softened her heart; perhaps she would even be capable of some kind of maternal gesture. Curiosity, hope; and a kind of dark attraction. I had succumbed and, as though afraid of changing my mind, I had immediately informed Frau Freihorst of my impending arrival.

I'm going to see you again today, mother, and my heart is pounding. What am I going to say to you? And if, as happened in 1971, you only want to talk about yourself and your past? So gratifying to make yourself heard after the collapse of Nazism, as though you had been simply erased. Will you try, as you did then, to praise your former comrades, some of whom, you told me, were 'irreproachable family men'?

I remember you mentioned the name of Rudolf Höss. You bragged about having known him well, and

7

also of having known and socialised with his wife and their five children. You said that Höss was the best commandant in Auschwitz, and that you were very sorry when he was transferred. You could no longer visit Frau Höss in her charming little house in the SS estate beyond the electrified perimeter fence – the same one that so many prisoners tried to hurl themselves against, hoping for a quick and liberating death. You could no longer recover your strength in the Höss family's idyllic little house, you couldn't shake off the exhaustion which, from time to time, prostrated even such a robust guard as yourself.

I have subsequently had the opportunity to read the memoirs that Höss wrote in the months leading up to his trial and execution, and I found myself thinking once more – with a mixture of dismay and disbelief – about the grandiloquence of your account of things. But perhaps, mother, perhaps you've changed now. Perhaps we'll finally be able to talk like a mother and a daughter who haven't seen each other for twenty-seven years – who have never spoken to each other, for a whole lifetime.

From a sworn affidavit by Rudolf Höss, member of the SS and Auschwitz camp commandant from 1st May 1940 until 1 December 1943, who was tried and sentenced to death by a Polish court:

'The mass-executions using gas began in the summer of 1941 and lasted until autumn 1944. I personally oversaw the executions in Auschwitz until 1 December 1943 [...]

'The "Final Solution" of the Jewish question meant the extermination of all the Jews in Europe.

'In 1942 I received the order to make the executions in Auschwitz more efficient. At the time there were already three other extermination camps in occupied Poland: Belzec, Treblinka and Wolzec. Those camps were under the command of the Security Police and the SD, the Reich's security and espionage service.

'I travelled to Treblinka to inspect their method of extermination. The commandant of the *Lager* told me that over the course of six months he had liquidated 80,000 people, most of them Jews from the Warsaw ghetto. He employed carbon monoxide, but in my opinion the method was not very efficient. So when I established the extermination process in Auschwitz I used Zyklon B, a crystallised Prussic acid which was thrown into the gas chambers through small openings. Death took between three and fifteen minutes. When the cries of the people could no longer be heard we knew that they were all dead.

'Another improvement over Treblinka was the construction of gas chambers which could accommodate up to 2,000 people, while the ten gas chambers in Treblinka had a total capacity of only 200.

'The method of selection of the victims was this: in Auschwitz two doctors were entrusted with the task of examining the new prisoners, who arrived at frequent intervals. The prisoners had each to pass in front of one of the doctors, who indicated his decision by nodding his head. Those who were fit for work were sent to the camp, and the rest were immediately dispatched to the extermination building. Young children were, without exception, exterminated as unfit for work.

'One final improvement on Treblinka was the following: while the victims of Treblinka almost always knew that they were going to be exterminated, in Auschwitz we sought to deceive them by making them think they were going to be disinfected for lice. In many cases, of course, they guessed our true intentions, and consequently we had to suppress a number of revolts. Mothers would often attempt to hide their little children under their clothes, but they were easily found, and sent immediately to the gas chambers. We should really have carried out the extermination in great secrecy, but the foul and nauseating stench from the ceaseless cremation of the bodies permeated the whole area, so the people who lived in the surrounding villages became aware that a process of extermination was under way in Auschwitz...'[1]

It's an unbearable thought, mother, those little children being separated from their mothers to be sent on their own to the gas chambers.

An unbearable thought: that my own mother was involved in all that.

[1] *Die Waffen-SS*, Rowohlt, Berlin, 1998, text and documentation by Wolfgang Schneider.

Sluggish and desolate rain; the tarmac on the road in front of the hotel flickers uncertainly in the light from the streetlamp, still lit.

Gradually, as the uncertain dawn reluctantly drags itself into a damp morning, I start to become aware that I am extremely tired; but my mind is wide awake, teeming with disturbing thoughts. I could do with a coffee, a good strong Italian-style coffee.

I'm going to see you again today, mother, and the prospect opens up a great gulf in the pit of my stomach. Twenty-seven years have passed since we last met. Will there still be anything to salvage, mother? Surely there's still something we can do – even if it's only to try to understand, to forgive; to attempt to forge an appallingly belated relationship between mother and daughter, however flimsy it might be.

'Hold your hands open,' you said. I'll never forget that. You had dragged me by one arm, as though to tell me a secret, into the bedroom of the little flat in the suburb of Mariahilf, and you had opened a little box. It's a standard gesture, one that usually heralds a present of some kind, don't you think, mother?

'Hold your hands open.' And then you filled them with rings, bracelets, cufflinks, pendants, brooches, a watch and a handful of necklaces, large and small. For a moment I looked uncomprehendingly at all that gold. Then I understood, and it was as though my hands were on fire. I pulled my palms apart, and the jewels clattered to the floor. You stared at me, puzzled.

'I wanted to give you a present,' you said finally, with frank ferocity. 'They might come in useful on a rainy day, you can never tell where life will take you.'

'I don't want them,' I replied.

Then you started to gather them all up, one by one, sadly and fastidiously. When you delicately picked up a little chain my heart plummeted.

It was one of those chains that you give to little girls on their fourth or fifth birthdays, an apparently slight little thing, but precious nonetheless. At that moment, with icy clarity, an image superimposed itself over the sight of you picking up all your gold: the image of you driving the little girl who had owned the necklace into the gas chamber. And in that moment everything was decided. I was sure of one thing: I didn't want this mother.

The mother who had never gone in search of me, and who was now ignoring my son, who sat alone in the living room with a colouring book.

I still remember your vexed disappointment: how could I, your daughter, refuse a gift like that? But really, mother, did you think you could compensate me for your long absence with a handful of gold?

'Are you really sure you don't want it?' you tried one last time. Such obtuse, exasperating insistence! 'No,' I said again. I didn't even try to explain why. There would have been no point.

I'm ready. All I have left to do is to go down to the lobby where Eva, my cousin, is waiting for me. She's come specially from Germany to be with me today. I'm suddenly tempted to cancel my visit, but it wouldn't be fair to try and make her an accomplice of such an act of childish cowardice. She has a sweet nature, but she's extremely predictable in her actions.

Eva is the daughter of my father Stefan's sister; we met up again a few years ago after a very long separation.

The last time I saw her was in 1942, in Berlin, where her parents had a magnificent villa frequented by the *crème de la crème* of the capital. It had been on the occasion of my father's second marriage, to Ursula, a young and ambitious woman from Berlin who had become my implacable enemy. She didn't want me; she would only accept Peter, my little brother. I repaid her rejection in kind. It was an instinctive, animal reaction.

My father had first met her when he was on leave, and, from what I was told, it was a classic *coup de foudre*. But it was also possible that one of his reasons for deciding to request a divorce and rush into this rather hasty marriage was to give his small children a second mother; their other mother, their real one, had left a year previously, in the autumn of 1941. I was four years old, and Peter was nineteen months. Our mother had abandoned us to join the SS. Left on our own, we had been taken in by Aunt Margarete, my father's sister. But given my aunt's precarious health, that could only be a temporary solution. Grandmother would have been happy to bring us up, but she was old, and it was thought better for the two children to grow up around a young woman who still had all her strength. The argument was theoretically flawless, but in practice it turned out to be a disaster.

After his sudden incursion into married life, my father went back to the front; from the very first, life with our stepmother was hell. Within a short time she got rid of me by locking me up in an institution for difficult children, a kind of storehouse for children whose families didn't want to have them under their feet, and once I was there I almost starved myself to death, unable to see any other way of escaping that desperate, horrific place.

'How do you feel?' Eva asks me. We're having breakfast in a quiet room whose windows look out on to a tree-lined courtyard, choked by smokiness and damp.

'Dreadful,' I reply, casting a resentful glance at the Italian-made espresso machine which produces anything you could imagine except an Italian-style coffee. 'I'd give anything for a decent cup of coffee,' I sigh.

'You've had three,' she reminds me.

'Dishwater,' I complain.

'I can't believe how devoted you Italians are to your coffee,' my cousin smiles. In her eyes, by now, I'm 'the Italian'.

'And you to your "*Würstel*",' I reply, although without acrimony: I love Eva, and despite the passing of the years I feel as close to her as if she were my sister.

'Chin up,' she encourages me. 'I'm here.'

'It's going to be a shock,' I predict. 'She'll have aged a lot. I might not even recognise her.'

'Well,' she agrees with affectionate irony, 'that's how it is, mothers age.'

'It's one thing watching your own mother getting older day by day,' I protest irritably, 'and quite another to meet her almost for the first time when she's sixty, the second time when she's nearly ninety!'

'You're right,' she agrees thoughtfully, placing a sympathetic hand on mine. 'But you can't pull out now. And you never know, you might be happy after all . . .?'

'I feel sick,' I announce disconsolately.

The taxi is on time. I booked it in advance, because the home is outside Vienna.

The taxi driver is a man in his forties, broader than he is tall, with a sizeable beer belly. For a while we all listen to a cheerful polka by Smetana, no one saying a word. It's still drizzling, and the sky is leaden. The wipers squeak monotonously against the windscreen. I remember my mother's file; Eva and I got it out yesterday at the Wiesenthal Centre. It included a cv that was even more disturbing than I had expected: early activism in the National Socialist Party, then Sachsenhausen, Ravensbrück and finally Auschwitz-Birkenau. In the women's concentration camp at Ravensbrück she had collaborated on certain experiments which were carried out on the prisoners, and then she had undergone the training for future extermination camp guards. The hardest, the toughest of them all, had been sent to Birkenau.

We are driving through the outskirts of Vienna. All of a sudden Eva asks the taxi driver to stop outside a florist's shop.

'Flowers?' I ask suspiciously.

'You're not going to turn up empty-handed?'

'Isn't that a bit hypocritical?'

'Sometimes you really have to make formal gestures,' she declares with implacable sweetness.

Shortly afterwards the taxi driver pulls up outside a flower shop. The interior is entirely clad in pale wood, and emanates a strong cemetery smell.

'What flowers were you thinking of?' Eva asks in a practical voice.

'I wasn't thinking of any kind of flowers,' I reply sulkily.

'Fine, then I'll take care of it.'

She chooses sober flowers, not too showy, and when the bouquet is ready she nods to the assistant to hand them to me. I take them almost with revulsion, as though they concealed something dangerous. I feel them pricking my fingers.

'There are thorns,' I protest.

The assistant, a woman with camomile-coloured hair tied at the back of her neck with a velvet ribbon, and eyes of an intense blue, looks offended.

'There aren't any thorns,' she replies.

'But . . .' I stammer.

'That's enough nonsense,' Eva whispers to me.

We pay and go. I turn around, and see that the florist is peering after us through the glass door of the shop.

'Thorns . . .' laughs Eva with a mixture of affection and irony.

We turn up a quarter of an hour early for our appointment, which has been arranged for ten o'clock.

The taxi stops by a big gate: on the other side of an old medieval-looking wall I can see a complex of pale buildings. The taxi driver opens the door, wishes us '*einen schönen Tag*', slides his beer belly back into his vehicle and drives away.

We are about to advance up the drive when all of a sudden I feel as though I'm choking.

'Stop . . .' I whisper.

'What's wrong?' Eva asks, worried.

'I can't breathe.'

'Take deep breaths, it's all the emotion.'

'I'm not emotional,' I maintain. I'm paralysed with panic.

I step back from the gate and lean against the trunk of an old plane tree. I'm confused, and furious with myself. I could have avoided all of this just by ignoring the letter. Now, as I gradually get my breath back, I'm thinking about how to get myself out of this, and go back the way I have come.

'Are you ready?' asks Eva.

'No,' I reply, kicking the tree that was supporting me.

All of a sudden I'm seized by a violent fit of coughing. I cough until tears come to my eyes.

'What's . . . happening . . . to me?' I sob. I open my handbag to look for a handkerchief, but the entire contents tumble out on to the wet grass. In a moment I'm really going to burst into tears.

Eva bends over to help me pick up my knickknacks; all of a sudden we're staring into each other's eyes.

'Do you remember what you said to me in 1942, in Berlin, when we last saw one another?' I ask, balancing on my heels.

Eva frowns.

'I think I called you a stupid cow.

'That's right,' I reply. 'What prompted that?'

'You'd called me a stupid nanny goat!' she remembers.

We both burst out laughing.

'Just think, fifty-six years have passed since then . . .' I sigh, as our laughter subsides. I stand up with some difficulty, one hand on my back. 'We're old now . . .'

When I'm on my feet again, Eva studies me critically.

'What is it?' I ask suspiciously.

'You should do your face. You've got lipstick on your eyelids and eyeshadow on your lips.'

'*Wunderbar*,' I say, and get the requisite tools out of my bag: mirror, powderpuff, compact.

'Ready?' says Eva.

'No.'

'We're okay,' she observes dryly. 'There's just a few minutes to go.'

At the caretaker's lodge we ask for Fräulein Inge, as I was told to do when I phoned from Italy to announce my visit.

The porter, a sprightly beanpole with mousy whiskers, starts fiddling with an impressive-looking telephone switchboard.

'You see that beige building behind the fountain?' he says finally. 'Go over there and ask again at the desk inside.'

The tension, broken a moment ago by our laughter, starts gnawing at me again; naked and oppressive. And on top of that I feel ridiculous clutching that bunch of flowers.

'They're sticking into me,' I murmur, partly to reassure myself that my voice hasn't dried up in my throat. I feel parched, and the soles of my feet are itching.

'Wait,' I say to Eva, pulling on the sleeve of her overcoat.

'What is it now?' she says, looking like a loving and impatient sister.

'I've got to take my shoes off.'

'Your shoes?' she stammers in consternation.

'The soles of my feet are itching . . .' I say pleadingly. But Eva shakes her head.

'Just don't think about it. It'll go away.' And taking me by the arm she guides me towards a wide doorway.

'We're on time, it's ten o'clock now,' she observes with satisfaction.

Once we've crossed the threshold, we find ourselves facing a transparent cage occupied by two young women who look like air hostesses. One of them is working at a computer; I turn to the other one and give her my name, asking whether Fräulein Inge has by any chance been informed of my arrival.

She dials a number with her pink painted nails.

'She's coming,' she tells us with thoroughly professional politeness.

But she immediately turns away and her smile fades. Her colleague has drawn her attention to something that is showing up on the computer screen. They both stare at it, reading intently. Finally they turn around, glancing at me from below. I think I understand. I'm the ex-Nazi's daughter.

I become aware of a familiar feeling of unease. I approach the wall, pretending to look at a print showing a village on one of the fabulous lakes of the Austrian Salzkammergut, and think again of that time in Milan, two years ago.

I had been invited to take part in a commemoration of the fiftieth anniversary of the racial laws. The participants, in a theatre that was packed to the roof, included a historian, a writer, representatives of

Milan's cultural life, two people who had been deported to the Nazi extermination camps, and me – daughter of a guard at Auschwitz-Birkenau.

During a break, a woman survivor from Birkenau came over to me. She stared right into my eyes, then exploded: 'I hate you!'

I was speechless for a moment.

'Why? Why do you hate me?' I asked, once I had recovered myself.

'Because your mother was a guard at Birkenau, and I even think I remember her. She was a heavy-handed blonde who once knocked out one of my front teeth with a truncheon. That was her, wasn't it? A tall, strapping blonde . . .' And she stared at me with resentful aggression.

'I don't . . . I don't know,' I stammered.

'You don't know whether your mother was blonde or not? You must have a photograph, something! I want to know, I want to know if that blonde in Birkenau was your mother!'

She had gripped me by one arm and her nervous fingers contracted around my wrist.

I shook my head impotently.

'I couldn't say. When my mother was in Birkenau I had no contact with her. I . . . I . . .' My voice died in my throat.

'It doesn't matter.' The woman loosened her grip, her hand fell back. 'Forgive me . . .'

She fell silent, and her shoulders bent in a strange and apparently painful movement.

She was about seventy, small and fragile, her face marked by ancient, ineradicable suffering.

One of the organisers, who had been observing the scene, came over: 'Quite honestly, I don't think that this is the place . . .' he began.

'You're right,' the woman interrupted him, her shoulders more and more bent over. 'I'm sorry . . . I couldn't help myself. Forgive me.' And she made to return to the stage. But then I clutched her arm and looked into her eyes. 'You have nothing to ask forgiveness for,' I said, 'but neither do you have any accusation to level at me. I was seven and a half when the war ended.'

Something softened in her face.

'Seven and a half . . .' she repeated. 'You're right. Forgive me once again.'

And she slipped away.

'You have to understand them,' commented the academic who had intervened in my defence, watching her as she left. 'They'll never be able to forget.'

'I know,' I answered.

No one who was in the camps has ever entirely left them. No Auschwitz survivor has ever been healed once and for all of the effects of evil.

'Are you waiting for me, ladies?' asked a young, clear voice. Fräulein Inge is a woman in her thirties with a round face, pink and cherubic.

We exchange our first few pleasantries.

'So, you haven't seen your mother for twenty-seven years?' She smiles, not a hint of reproach in her voice.

I reply with some difficulty, swallowing hard. It's as though my vocal cords are paralysed.

'Yes . . . But of course there are reasons for that . . .

I mean, it might sound strange for a daughter . . .'

Fräulein Inge gently shakes her head. 'You don't have to justify yourself, it's a strictly private matter.'

I appreciate her discretion, but at the same time I feel frustrated. I wanted to explain.

I wonder what the people in there know about my mother.

'I'd like to ask you something,' I finally manage to articulate. 'Has . . . has my mother kept her past a secret, or . . . ?'

'Nothing of the sort,' she replies. 'But it isn't a problem, believe me.'

'So my mother talks to the others about it?'

'Sometimes.'

'And . . .' I swallow hard again.

'. . . how do they react?' She smiles, almost tenderly. 'Many of them – including your mother, by the way – have difficulty remembering things. After an hour they've forgotten it all again.'

'There's one more thing I'd like to ask.' My heart is knocking loudly against my ribs.

'Please ask anything you like.'

'How does my mother talk about her children?'

Fräulein Inge replies in a neutral voice.

'When she came here she announced that her children had abandoned her, but a few days later she revised her version of things and said that they were both dead. She has continued to believe that until today.'

I glimpse a flicker of cowardly hope.

'Mightn't it be dangerous for her mental health to see me appearing as if out of nowhere?' I suggest. 'Mightn't it give her a shock?'

Fräulein Inge smiles faintly.

'Haven't you spoken to the doctor who's dealing with your mother?' she asks discreetly. I can't deny it.

'Yes, I have. And he said that . . . that there were no contraindications.'

'Fine,' she replies, putting a hand on my shoulder, 'in that case I have no contraindications either. I'll walk you in.'

'Just one more minute,' I say quickly. Panic has me by the throat.

'Is there anything else you want to ask me?' Fräulein Inge says. Her diplomatic tone is disarming: she has registered my desperate ploy to gain some time.

'How is she?' I ask. 'I mean, physically.'

'Your mother is reasonably well. Admittedly she's not getting any younger. She has her ailments, but nothing at all serious.'

'And mentally?'

'It varies from day to day. But she's undergoing treatment. They're trying to improve her memory and to encourage her to socialise.'

'Does she have problems socialising?'

'Well . . . your mother can be a little difficult.'

'In what sense?'

Fräulein Inge ushers us over to a window; we're blocking the corridor.

'Sometimes she's cheerful,' she continues, 'and she talks and jokes with the others and with the staff. She talks about her past, and often about the years she has spent with her friend Frau Freihorst. She also talks about her time in prison and . . . yes, sometimes she feels the need to remember those times. I mean . . . the camps. In fact, when she addresses that subject, she becomes extraordinarily lucid, although the following day she can't remember a single word she said.'

There's a pause. The air in the corridor is hot and a little stuffy.

'May I open the window for a moment?' I ask with a gasp.

'Of course,' she says. 'Aren't you feeling well?'

'Just a little tense.'

She opens the window, a heavy, high nineteenth-century window, and for a moment I lean out, with my elbows on the broad sill.

The air is moist but not cold, and the scent of the damp vegetation brings me a feeling of relief. A black-bird perches on the branch of a young larch, watched closely by a sparrow with ruffled feathers.

I pull myself together, draw myself back inside and close the window.

'I'm ready,' I announce. But I'm not entirely sure.

We go up to the top floor and emerge into a wide corridor full of moving people. Nurses, doctors, visiting relations, serving staff. Groups of armchairs and coffee tables are arranged along a wall enlivened by colourful prints. Two ladies are involved in an animated discussion, others are reading the paper or knitting, some are talking on mobile phones.

Fräulein Inge stops a colleague and asks her about my mother. Her colleague, a tall, chubby, baby-faced girl, opens her eyes wide, looks around and exclaims, in puzzlement, 'But I saw her not more than a second ago! Perhaps she's gone to the bathroom.'

'Excuse me one moment,' says Fräulein Inge,

popping her head into first one bathroom, then another. It's at that moment that I see her, in a corridor off to the side.

Rather than recognising her, I *feel* that it's my mother. That woman is my mother.

I'm aware of a kind of shiver running down my back, and my heart skips a beat.

How she's changed. I stare at her from a distance. How she's changed.

'What is it?' Eva whispers to me.

'I've seen her,' I answer hoarsely.

'Where is she?'

I point with my chin.

'That lady sitting by the window?'

At that moment Fräulein Inge comes back.

'I don't understand,' she announces, confused, 'I can't find her anywhere . . . Oh . . . yes, there she is.' And she brushes my arm sympathetically.

'I need to get my breath back,' I say, grasping for an excuse.

'I understand,' she replies. 'There's no rush. I understand what you're going through.'

I'm short of breath, and my forehead is covered in sweat. Eva grips my arm.

'Come on, I'm here . . .'

I raise my eyes, and summon up the strength to look at my mother again.

She's sitting in an armchair, absorbed in her thoughts, her arms resting on the armrests in an attitude of abandonment that touches my heart. The abandonment of a person who has disappeared, who is lost in a soundless and colourless void. She is immobile as though afraid that the slightest movement might suck her into a black and bottomless abyss. I feel disturbed, moved, powerless.

She is staring at a row of plane trees outside the window, but her expression is vacant. She is looking, but seeing nothing.

'Go on, go over to her, talk to her,' my cousin urges me affectionately.

But I feel as if I'm paralysed; my heart is pounding, and my knees are shaking. I'm panting, my eyes are misty.

No, I wasn't expecting this. I wasn't expecting that the mere sight of my mother would unsettle me like this. Will I ever be able to describe the sensations that are alternating within me at that moment, feelings that I can't hold back?

I take a deep breath and try to regain control of my nerves.

'Go on, go over to her,' Eva insists.

I take a few steps with difficulty. Then I purse my lips and, finally, walk resolutely towards my mother. I stop in front of her, forcing her to raise her eyes to look at me.

There, we're facing one another. She's old, thin – unbelievably fragile. She can't weigh more than seven stone. A woman who, twenty-seven years ago, was still a healthy, vigorous, robust woman. I can't suppress a feeling of infinite pity.

All of a sudden I'm struck by the very clear blue of her eyes. I didn't remember them being so blue. They study me glassily, icy and empty.

Her face is thin and pointed, her skin greyish and

transparent, her nose slender and sharp. And her body, even though she is sitting down, looks like an empty husk that might crumble at any moment. Her shoulders are graceful, her chest concave. All of a sudden I feel a visceral, biological anxiety at the sight of this simulacrum of my own future senility.

I lean forward slightly, I want to shatter that void in her eyes. I stay there with my eyes deep in hers: my mother's eyes.

A few minutes pass.

Finally, in the depths of those pupils, something awakens – an imperceptible flicker, an uncertain flame.

'I've seen you before,' she says, all of a sudden, in a voice that I don't remember: a senile voice, dry and porous.

My heart thumps in my throat.

'Are you my sister?' she asks, more to herself than to me. But she immediately dismisses the idea.

'No, she's dead,' she announces darkly, with a gesture that seems to want to chase away such an uncomfortable thought.

'I'm your daughter.'

'Who?' And she leans her head to one side, holding her ear as though trying to catch a distant echo. Then she shakes her head adamantly and announces in a cold voice, 'My daughter's dead too.'

Then she tilts her head, bends her shoulders and begins to stare at her fingers with exaggerated attention, as though she has never seen them before.

She has long, white hands, bony and ancient. I find them rather repellent. For a fraction of a second I'm ashamed of them, but there's nothing I can do about it: I didn't learn to love them as they withered.

'I'm your daughter,' I repeat, tearing my eyes away from her hands.

'NO!' she insists. 'My daughter died long ago.'

Then I lift her chin and say firmly and clearly, 'Look At Me, I Am Your Daughter!'

And without giving her time to deny it, I take my teddy bear from my bag and hold it in front of her eyes.

That moth-eaten teddy bear, a sad relic of early childhood, had been given to me the previous day by Frau Freihorst, my mother's friend.

Frau Freihorst was small and plump, with a serious, slightly prim expression, some years younger than my mother, and she smelled of cinnamon and Marseilles soap. She had given my cousin and myself an embarrassingly warm welcome in her old Viennese house full of trinkets and crocheted doilies.

She had known Traudi, she said – using the affectionate diminutive by which she always referred to her friend – for more than forty years, and she had never condemned her for her past, because she didn't consider it her place to judge. But she had observed with distress her slow mental deterioration, and it was the inexorable advance of her illness that had led her to write to me.

She showed us, not without a certain degree of mischief, lots of photographs of my mother and herself that had been taken during the years when they had still consorted with a group of men friends – widowers, divorcees, even some inveterate bachelors who were identifiable by the way they winked at the camera.

Her friendship with Traudi was one of those that you often come across, between people of very dissimilar, not to say opposite, temperaments: Frau Freihorst described my mother as 'terrible' and 'barking mad', but she had loved her vitality and resourcefulness, before old age had dulled them.

Their lives had taken very different courses, too: in contrast to my mother's fanaticism, Frau Freihorst had never been anything other than a dutiful citizen. She had lost a husband and two sons to Hitler's war. Otherwise, she was resigned to the events that had affected her and her country. 'We wanted it,' she admitted frankly. 'I was one of those who voted for the annexation of Austria, and when Hitler drove through Vienna in his open-topped Mercedes I threw him a bouquet of flowers.'

She repeatedly asked my forgiveness for writing to me. But she had written out of affection, she said. Perhaps she had been poking her nose into matters that were none of her concern, and anyway . . .

'Traudi isn't in good physical health,' she observed, with tears in her eyes, 'but you never know. At her age she could go to sleep one evening and never wake up again. And if you hadn't seen each other at least one last time . . .'

'I'm grateful to you, believe me,' I said, trying to reassure her in the most convincing tone I could manage.

Encouraged, Frau Freihorst began to tell me what had happened after my 1971 visit. My mother had begun to feel a sense of guilt – something that she had previously been unaware of – about myself, my brother and our father. At first her feelings merely irritated her, and she tried to shake them off; then, gradually, as though a tumour were growing in her body, she started behaving in a very strange way.

'What I mean,' the woman continued in a sad voice, 'is that she developed an impulse to rid her flat of everything that had anything to do with her ex-husband and her two children. Photographs, documents, objects.'

'How did she get rid of them?' I asked.

'She threw them all out into the dustbin, along with brand new goods.'

'Brand new?' I asked, bemused.

'Yes, it was all part of the ritual. She had to throw away your belongings along with objects that she'd just acquired. She bought all kinds of things, shoes and books, pyjamas and sets of plates, clothes and carpets. One day she came home with an enormous indoor cactus, which went the same way as everything else. Oh, and then there was a camera as well, you know, one of those cameras that take instant pictures. That ended up in the rubbish as well, and you can imagine the fuss there was in the neighbourhood. The rumour went around that your mother was throwing away new things, and there was this dreadful competition to see who could retrieve the most interesting and valuable objects from the bins. Two old ladies came to blows over that cactus, and one of them ended up on the ground with a terrible gash on her head. The footpath was covered with blood, it was a disgraceful performance. The ambulance turned up, and a crowd of people came to gawp. All for the sake of a stupid cactus.'

Frau Freihorst ignored my bewilderment.

'I don't know what you would call Traudi's behaviour in psychiatric terms, but in my view it was a funeral rite. In short, to rid herself of her sense of guilt, your mother was giving you, your brother and your father symbolic funerals. The dead make no demands on you, you know?'

'None of us ever planned to ask her for anything,' I objected.

'But she didn't know that. Who knows what kind of mess there was in that poor head of hers.'

'But then she calmed down?' I asked.

'Yes, but she needed treatment. I went along with her. She had to report to our district mental health service three times a week. It was at around this time that she also developed an obsession with cleaning.'

'What did she do?'

'She cleaned from morning till night. Her flat, I mean. She cleaned and cleaned, tipping up whole buckets of water over the floor and flooding the landing. She cleaned furiously, and there was nothing her social workers could do.'

'And what was the meaning of it all?'

Frau Freihorst shrugged her shoulders.

'Who knows? Perhaps she wanted to cleanse her past, sweep away . . . let's call them the nasty things. That phase lasted for about a year, and then it stopped from one day to the next. She went through a period of relative calm, and the Traudi that I knew seemed to come back. But then she started having problems with her short-term memory. At first there was the matter of the sugar.'

'Sugar?'

'Yes. She would buy it one day, and then she would buy it again the next day, and the day after that. She could accumulate up to ten kilos. The same thing happened with bread. One day I discovered an enormous quantity of it in a cupboard; she must have been buying kilos of bread every day, for at least a week. But then things got even worse. She would often leave her house and get lost. In her handbag she always carried a piece of paper with a message to phone me in case of an emergency. Have you any idea how many times I went to fetch her from the most unlikely places? One day, for example, she went into an undertaker's. She'd ordered a white coffin for a little girl, with all the trimmings you would have for a funeral. But then she wouldn't leave; she just sat there on a chair, silent and sulking. After a while they decided to call the police. Then she took out the piece of paper with my phone number on it. That time, as usual, I went and collected her in a taxi.' And she added with benevolent indulgence, 'Which she never paid me for.'

She thought for a moment.

'But I prefer to remember the times before her problems became quite so serious. Every now and again she would make me laugh. After the funeral rites, for example, she started talking about her children and about Stefan, her ex-husband, in the past tense. She said: perhaps it's a good thing that my daughter died prematurely, I wouldn't have been able to bear being the mother of . . .' She broke off with an embarrassed smile. 'No, I can't say it.'

'Go on,' I pleaded.

'She said she couldn't bear to be the mother of an *alte Schachtel*, an old bag.'

'She really said that?' I asked, a little hurt.

She nodded. 'Your mother was always a rather . . . a rather vain woman. She didn't want to grow old.'

My mother stares at the teddy bear with a mixture of astonishment and disbelief.

Then she says slowly, in a whining voice, 'This is Zakopane and you must have stolen him. He belonged to my daughter. Where did you get him?'

'I didn't steal him,' I answer, 'he belongs to me.'

'He belonged to my daughter!' she vehemently protests.

'I am your daughter.'

She shakes her head, and for a few moments she hides her face in her hands. From the shaking of her body I assume that she is crying, but she isn't. Uncovering her face she murmurs, serious and alert, 'His name is Zakopane because Stefan and I bought him in Zakopane in Poland. We were on our way to fetch . . .' But she's already having problems. 'We were on our way to fetch two people . . .'

'Your children, that's who you were going to fetch,' I say, coming to her aid. 'Your children, Helga and Peter.'

Berlin, July 1941. The second year of the war.

My grandparents were looking after a farm in Poland, fortunately for them as 'annexed Austrians' rather than natives. The Nazis saw the Poles as an inferior race, so much so that they forbade them to bury

33

their dead in consecrated ground. But they were afraid of the awkward local intelligentsia, and decided to wipe them out. A dear friend of my grandparents, for example, a politician with radical tendencies, was murdered outside the city hall in Wroclaw.

One day my grandmother paid us an unexpected visit in Berlin, to discover my brother and me being looked after by a stranger. The woman explained to her that 'the lady' – meaning my mother – was always very busy with her political affairs, which was why she often turned to her to look after her two 'little angels'. It was certainly not the first time that we had been given to strangers to be looked after, and our grandmother, who knew that, went through the roof: she paid the recalcitrant babysitter on the spot and told her she could go to the devil.

All afternoon my grandmother waited for my mother to come home. At about eleven o'clock in the evening there was an air-raid. We all went to the shelter, heavy with sleep.

At dawn my mother still hadn't come home. At about nine o'clock grandmother started making our breakfast: fortunately she had brought some provisions with her from Poland, because our larder was nearly empty. The milk was powdered, and I complained because I hated it. I vaguely remember my grandmother trying to explain it to me: the war, she said, imposed certain restrictions. More than her words, which I understood to a certain extent, it was her calm and undramatic tone of voice that calmed me down. At the time grandmother, hating the Führer and the Third Reich with all her heart, was still fairly optimistic about the outcome of the war, and she certainly didn't imagine the catastrophic fate that awaited us.

After breakfast she thought she might distract us by reading to us; she took us into my father's study – he was already at the front – in search of a book of fairy tales. There weren't any, but instead, in the middle of the room, there stood a cumbersome big box full of copies of *Mein Kampf*. It may have been my mother's task to distribute them: at the time the book was being widely disseminated among the German people, and young couples were even given copies as wedding presents from the state.

Grandmother picked up one of the volumes and, turning it around in her vigorous peasant hands, said, with extreme disdain, '*Pfui!*' It was a critical reaction which, had it been expressed in public, would at the very least have brought accusations of defeatism down on her head.

When my mother finally did come home, my grandmother greeted her with her face white with rage and her fists in the air. There was a frightening scene that made the walls shake. My mother came out of it almost paralysed: for the umpteenth time she had been found wanting by her mother-in-law, who had never concealed her aversion for my mother since her engagement to my father. Her attempts at self-justification fell on deaf ears. She tried in vain to explain that as a member of the SS, when the call came from the Reichsführer she had to jump.

Grandmother, who had already made the basic preparations, took Peter and me and brought us with her to Poland.

* * *

All of a sudden my mother starts staring at me with a cautious expression. I smile at her, but her face is grave. She actually presses her arm tighter around her chest as though in an instinctive gesture of fear. A tremor runs through her limbs, the muscles of her face stiffen and her lips curl into a series of grimaces.

'Who are you?' she asks finally, in a dark and anxious voice.

'I am your daughter,' I repeat calmly.

With a surprisingly agile movement she grabs the teddy bear out of my hand and presses it to her cheek.

'We bought him in Zakopane,' she murmurs after making a slow and laborious effort of memory, 'along with . . . something else.' She comes to a standstill.

'A toy squirrel for Peter,' I say, coming to her assistance again.

She nods as though in her sleep. 'Yes, a squirrel. We had gone to fetch the children. My mother-in-law had taken them away, you see? And she sent a telegram to Stefan, that harpy did. And Stefan had to ask for his leave that wasn't due until Christmas, and we went to take the children back. Stefan was furious, but it was all his mother's fault. She hated me and I hated her. And then . . .'

She takes one last glance at the teddy bear and puts it in one of the pockets of her woollen suit, the colour of a soldier's uniform.

'Peter's dead,' she declares, staring at me grimly.

I decide not to correct her for the moment. Instead I ask, in an almost sad voice, 'Do you really not remember me?'

She shakes her head, stubbornly, irritably. But a

shaky little smile begins to spread around her lips.

'Are you Helga?'

I nod, touched.

I would have liked to be able to answer, 'Yes, mum,' but there would have been no point in even trying. We aren't used to it. The last time I called her 'mum' was when I was four years old, and since then I have never said the word: '*Mutti*'. My stepmother was insistent that I should call her that. She would yell, 'Now I am your mother and you must call me *Mutti*!' I couldn't help it; however much I tried, I couldn't say that word. And she punished me. She sent me to bed without any supper: 'You can eat when you've called me *Mutti*'. Or else she would lock me up all day, in the dark, in my father's study. Or beat me with a stick. She tried everything she could think of, but she could never get me to say *Mutti*. I was stubborn, and I didn't want her. I didn't want my stepmother. I wanted my grandmother, who had looked after me and Peter after our mother had left. I rejected my stepmother, who from the start had only ever loved cuddly, happy little Peter, and she had never concealed the fact. She wouldn't even show me love when things were at their worst, not even when the situation in Berlin became insupportable and we were forced to spend months locked up in the cellar with all the other tenants of the building, with no drinking water, no light, no running water and only a small amount of rationed food of appalling quality.

One morning, down in that hell, we all discovered that we were covered with red boils. We found that our straw mattresses were infested with bed bugs. Even in that awkward situation my stepmother demonstrated her rejection, not to say her loathing of me. In fact she did everything she could think of to keep me from using the precious ointment that eased the terrible itching: she said it had to do for everyone in the cellar. So, unlike everyone else, I went on furiously scratching myself.

This came to the attention of her father, my grandfather by marriage (I called him *Opa*, grandfather). He registered what was going on and flew into a rage; he furiously attacked his daughter, using, for the first time, very harsh words, calling her 'perfidious' and 'despicable'. My stepmother was obliged to treat me. I was still the last to stop scratching. I had been in serious danger, and *Opa* realised that: in a situation like ours, without medicines and in atrocious hygienic conditions, those wounds could have gone septic, and might even have been fatal.

'Helga's dead too,' says my mother, but her voice sounds less certain now. She looks at me: 'Are you Helga?'

'Yes,' I answer for the third time. 'I'm Helga, your daughter.'

And once again I'd love to add the word *Mutti*, but I can't.

The only person I ever addressed in that way in my life was Frau Heinze, the headmistress of Eden College, the boarding school in which my stepmother imprisoned me while the war was raging, on the pretext that I was mischievous and insubordinate. I was permitted to call her *Mutti* Heinze, and I did so with enthusiasm because she was good to us, even if

she was strict. In the evening she sang us Brahms's
Lullaby:

> *Guten Abend, gute Nacht,*
> *Mit Röslein bedacht,*
> *Mit Näglein besteckt.*
> *Schlüpf' unter die Deck'* . . .

All of a sudden my mother leans towards me and
narrows her eyes. I can smell her old woman's smell.
Her hair smells of honey, it must be her shampoo. At
last she slowly brushes one of my cheeks as strange
noises emerge from her mouth, as though she were
counting, or whispering something learned from
memory.

'Helga!' she shouts all of a sudden.

She leaps backwards. 'It's Helga! My daughter's
here! It's really her, look!' she announces at the top of
her voice.

And she leans forward and fidgets and gesticulates
disjointedly like a crazed puppet.

'Come here!'

Now she is screeching in an undignified manner; a
number of curious onlookers come discreetly over to
us.

She nods to me, and sobs and laughs, and is stunned
and confused, and the onlookers smile, with some
amusement and a little unease.

But all of a sudden she falls silent, leans her head on
her forearm and starts crying her heart out. Her whole
body shakes. She weeps with the naked, oblivious
abandon of a child. The faces of the people watching

us are a picture of perplexity and embarrassment. I try to distract her.

'You remember Eva?'

My mother lifts her head and immediately stops crying, as though someone has pressed a button.

'Eva?' she repeats.

'My cousin,' I explain.

'Your cousin?' Her hands wave around in disbelief.

'Exactly,' I reply. 'Eva from Berlin.'

My mother fixes her eyes on Eva. There isn't a trace of benevolence in her expression. With a note of hostility in her voice she remembers, 'They were very rich people.' Then, almost with respect, she adds, more thoughtfully this time, 'He was in the Party.'

She reflects, then floors Eva with a question: 'Is it true that your father was in the Party and belonged to the SA from the time of the Stahlhelm?'

Eva is thrown. She would never have expected such a direct assault. But she replies, with admirable presence of mind: 'No, my father was never in the SA.'

'But he was in the Party!' my mother insists.

Eva makes a barely perceptible nod of assent.

'And he co-owned a factory with a Jew!' my mother proclaims triumphantly. 'What was the Jew's name?'

I don't like the turn that the conversation is taking; I try to change the subject.

'You remember Eva's mother? You know that Eva has a photograph with you in it too, wearing a wonderful hat, in the garden at their villa?'

'Am I standing next to Margarete?' she asks with a frown.

'Yes.'

'Margarete never liked me much,' she declares resentfully. 'But you know, in those days people were suspicious about Party activists.'

She's clearly thinking of herself, but decides it would be indulgent to dwell on the subject and asks, 'But how are you? You must be very old by now.'

Eva says nothing, taken aback. And in any case, how could she be expected to reply? By telling my mother that immediately after the war, in Berlin, her own mother was raped by four Russians in front of her? That her mother had been left with permanent psychological damage, and shortly afterwards had taken her own life with forty Veronal tablets?

'So,' my mother insists, 'how is old Margarete? Wrinkles and false teeth?'

She cackles cruelly, and I feel a sense of disgust. A moment later she strikes a hand to her forehead and shrieks, 'Silberberg! Silberberg was the name of the Jew your father owned the factory with, the factory that produced . . . wait . . . I can't remember. But am I right?'

I'm repelled by her insinuating and malevolent tone.

'And after the Nuremberg Laws your father threw him out of the factory, isn't that right?'

Eva has turned white.

'I wasn't born at the time,' she manages to reply. I admire her self-control.

'But he did throw that fellow Silberberg out, didn't he? Your father must have spoken to you about it at one time or another. He was a loyal member of the Party, don't ever forget that, my dear.'

She is agitated now, she wants to get to the nub of

the matter. I am growing exasperated. My hands start itching, and then I remember I'm still holding those damned flowers in my left hand. I hand them to her.

She seems to explode with joy: she erupts into a series of little sobbing cries, and displays the bouquet to the curious spectators, of whom there are now quite a crowd. I feel as though I'm at the centre of a stage, the involuntary protagonist of an inferior melodrama. The scene strikes me as vulgar and absurd. Nothing is as I had imagined it. I wish I was somewhere else, I wish I'd never come here. This woman, my mother, doesn't deserve the trouble I have taken, she's not worthy of my good intentions.

I look at her: now she is pulling some of the flowers from the bunch and throwing them to the onlookers; senile and pathetic, cruel and romantic. That was how Himmler's blackshirts were, including women like herself, the SS in skirts.

A dull sense of unease grips the pit of my stomach. The air is stale, I need oxygen.

Fräulein Inge must have read my mind: she goes and opens the window. But all of a sudden my mother turns around, stares at Eva and shouts, radiantly: 'That's where I saw that man Silberberg again! In the camp! When he arrived, he dared to use my name at the *Aufnahmebaracke*, can you imagine?'

She looks around as though expecting a burst of applause.

'He used my name because we once bumped into each other at your villa,' and here she glances accusingly at Eva, 'in the mistaken belief that it might ensure more considerate treatment for his daughter, it might even save her from the rat poison!' And she cackles shrilly, winking at the bystanders.

I know the story.

Silberberg had been transported to Birkenau with his aged parents, his gravely ill wife and their three children of five, six and thirteen. The oldest, Edith, was sent to be a forced labourer in a munitions factory near the *Lager*. She survived Auschwitz, and Eva had had an emotional reunion with her in Berlin in 1968. After the war she had married a music teacher, who watched gently over her nightmare-torn nights. The ghost of Birkenau would not leave her be. For a long time she couldn't hold down any kind of food, and suffered from serious panic attacks. Before finding a semblance of serenity, she had to undergo a course of psychotherapy that lasted for years.

Her father, after arriving in Birkenau, had been sent to one of the feared sub-camps, where he died. Many of the inmates worked underground, opening up galleries in the rocky walls. The clothing and food were scant and inferior, hygiene was appalling, the risk of typhus was extremely high, and cholera and petechial fever wiped out the workforce over the course of a few months. Silberberg's parents, his sick wife and his two younger children were immediately sent to the gas chambers.

I am already exhausted, and glance guiltily at Fräulein Inge – who all at once takes control of the situation. First of all she asks the onlookers to move away, after which she tries to take my mother by surprise with diversionary tactics.

'Why don't you show me that?' she asks, pointing at the teddy bear sticking out of the bag.

'No, it's mine!' my mother protests with the obstinacy of a child.

'Just for a moment,' Fräulein Inge insists with a smile.

'Won't!' she repeats crossly.

And all of a sudden she changes tack. She turns to me with a sweet and disarming expression, smiles and tries to coax me.

'I can keep it, can't I?' she asks, gesturing with her head towards the teddy bear. No, I don't want her to keep it, I don't want her to have it.

Fräulein Inge acts as though to take it out of the bag, but my mother, with a swiftness that surprises me, grabs her arm.

'Ah, you see, you can't trick me, I'm not decrepit yet!'

In the confusion, however, the teddy bear has ended up on the floor. My mother stares at it anxiously. 'Pick him up, someone, I want him! He's mine, I don't want anyone else to have him.'

Eva leans forward and hands it to her. My mother takes advantage of the situation to address her reproachfully: 'So you're Eva, Ludwig and Margarete's daughter?'

She looks her insolently up and down.

'Yes,' she concedes, 'you were very pretty as a girl, but you're old now.'

I feel my irritation mounting; I'd like to intervene but I can't.

'Your mother was very pretty too,' she continues,

apparently having recovered her memory all of a sudden, 'but she was vain. She had her breasts reduced, but in those days the doctors weren't terribly good at things like that. The surgeon was an idiot, and he left her with horrible scars. They leaked pus after the operation.'

She cackles. 'I certainly had no need of that, and in any case, I've always been absolutely terrified of hospitals.'

She leans her head forward, runs her tongue over her purple lips. She changes the subject: 'What happened to your villa?'

'It was bombed,' Eva replies.

'Oh yes, I remember: your father had Speer's bunker built on your property.'

That was true, it was thanks to Speer's bunker that Eva, her mother, two of their servants and their cat Berny had managed to survive.

It was a small and attractive construction, designed to protect anyone inside from the force of the bombing. The plans were drawn by Albert Speer himself, the Führer's architect, then his Minister of Munitions. Of course it was very expensive, and only very wealthy people could have afforded it.

My mother, who is well aware of this, sniggers: 'If your father hadn't been rich, you wouldn't be here today.' And she gives Eva a hard shove on the shoulder.

Suddenly she frowns. 'Speer, the traitor,' she explodes, full of rancour. 'He should have been hanged, and instead he got off with a prison sentence.' Her mood is rapidly darkening, as though the case had only just been reported.

'And he wanted to suffocate the Führer, and everyone else in the bunker,' she goes on furiously. She has slipped into the past tense without noticing.

It is true, Speer did contemplate killing Hitler by introducing a lethal gas into the bunker's ventilation pipes. And every time I hear this mentioned, I shiver to think that at the start of December 1944, through the good offices of aunt Hilda, my stepmother's sister who worked at the Ministry of Propaganda, my brother and I spent several days in that bunker as 'special guests of the Führer'.

A few seconds later my mother abruptly changes tack. She pierces poor Eva with her gaze and returns to a subject that clearly obsesses her.

'How old are you, my dear?' And, hearing the response, she exclaims, 'As old as that?' with evident disgust.

It's too much.

'Eva and I are the same age, you know that,' I intervene with a certain severity.

She looks me up and down, disappointed; her face darkens. 'It can't be. I don't want that. I can't have a daughter as old as that!' She glances down at her own body. 'I'm still beautiful, I'm not decrepit in the slightest. How could I have a daughter who looks like an old bag?'

Fräulein Inge pulls her up short: 'You mustn't be rude to your guests.'

'I was just telling the truth,' she replies, offended. 'I was just saying what I thought. Is there some sort of law against that?'

She throws the flowers to the floor.

'And I don't want those flowers! I'm not dead yet, and I don't want those flowers. They aren't even my favourites – I only like yellow roses.'

She falls silent, with a sulky grimace, the teddy bear clutched tightly in her hand. And all of a sudden she asks me a question: 'Do you like my clothes?' Caught unawares, I nod mechanically.

'Do you like the colour?'

'Yes,' I lie.

'It's the same colour as my uniform,' she announces. Then she leans towards me and whispers, 'I sent it to the comrades; you know where, don't you?' She stares at me with an air of complicity.

I reply with what's supposed to be a non-committal nod. I had seen my mother's SS uniform at her house, in 1971. She had taken it out of the wardrobe with solemn nostalgia, asking me to try it on. I had refused.

'All my suits are that colour,' she continues, as if by way of small talk. 'That one's the nicest.'

Meanwhile Fräulein Inge has picked up the flowers and put them in a vase.

'Now,' she says, 'you'd be better off moving to the guest room, where you can talk to each other in peace.'

My mother protests. 'No, I don't want to go there. It's a nasty room, nasty and cold.'

'It's neither nasty nor cold,' replies Fräulein Inge, 'and apart from anything else you always go there with your friend.'

'I have no friends!'

'Isn't Frau Freihorst your friend?'

My mother makes a contemptuous gesture: 'She's nothing.'

'You shouldn't treat loyal friends like that,' Fräulein Inge says disapprovingly.

'Pffff! I'm not going into that room because that's where I felt ill, I had a heart attack.'

Fräulein Inge smiles indulgently. 'You've never had a heart attack, thank the Lord.'

'Of course I have. I nearly died.'

I glance, puzzled, at Fräulein Inge, who explains, 'She'd just stuffed herself on ice cream, it was indigestion.'

'That's not true!' shrieks my mother, outraged.

'You mustn't tell lies,' the Fräulein replies severely. 'And that's enough of your nonsense now, I'm going to go with you to the guest room.' And, gripping my mother's wrist, she invites Eva and me to follow her.

The minute we're inside, my mother digs in her heels like a mule and scrutinises me grimly. 'What did you do with the teddy bear?' she says.

When Frau Freihorst had opened the door of my mother's apartment, my heart had skipped a beat. I had emerged from that flat twenty-seven years previously, convinced that I would never set foot there again, and yet here I was, crossing that threshold once more.

We walked into the hall, then into the sitting room.

There was the table where my son had sat, five years old at the time, with his crayons and a colouring book that my mother had given him, as well as a glass of milk and a pile of chocolate biscuits arranged on a big plate with a decorated border.

The same furniture as before, and cloths draped over the white armchairs. The sight chilled me. I looked around with a combination of dismay and revulsion; and yet there was something obscurely familiar about the place. All of a sudden I had the feeling that I was suffocating. Frau Freihorst hurried to open a window. I breathed deeply, and stood there for a moment looking down at the courtyard below.

It was a narrow Viennese courtyard, bare and unadorned. Nineteenth-century windows were set in the cracked walls, their sills decorated here and there with pots of evergreens.

An old man with long, white hair, sitting on a tiled surface above the gas meters, was eating a sandwich wrapped in a sheet of newspaper, every now and again throwing crumbs to a group of sparrows.

'Are you all right?' asked Eva, beside me.

'I'm a bit thrown,' I replied.

'Would you like to have a look at the bedroom?' I heard Frau Freihorst saying behind me. I nodded.

The minute I walked in I was struck by an atmosphere of icy solitude. I was chilled to the bone, and felt as though I were violating someone's private property. And that, indeed, was what I was doing: my mother would never know of this intrusion.

The room was orderly, but neurotically so, with the kind of pedantic and sterile order that seems final and irrevocable. The head of the household had gone, the dust could take over again.

I looked around with a mixture of curiosity and unease. My mother's furniture, her things. The wardrobe in which she kept her SS uniform. And then there was a chest with three big drawers, a little inlaid dressing table, a broad bed with an immaculate chenille counterpane, and long curtains of fine fabric on both windows. A walnut bookcase held several volumes, including some highly respectable titles.

Frau Freihorst explained that my mother was an assiduous reader. 'She even read in . . .' She broke off and blushed slightly.

I encouraged her with a slightly forced smile.

'She read in Birkenau,' she went on with the embarrassment of someone expressing something that might sound paradoxical. And no one could say that reading in Birkenau wasn't a paradox.

I didn't want to investigate my mother's passion for reading any further. I turned my back on the bookcase, and my eye fell on a painting depicting a sunset over a lake. It was rather impressively done. Frau Freihorst explained, almost in the tone of a guide showing people around a museum: 'Many years ago your mother invested in figurative art. She had around ten paintings that were worth a fair bit of money, but one day burglars got in and took the lot. This is the only picture she has bought since then. She couldn't resist the intensity of the light. She bought it and had it insured, because it's by quite a well-known painter.'

'So she didn't have financial problems,' I murmured, almost distractedly.

Frau Freihorst hesitated for a moment, and then said, 'I think you ought to know: since she was released from prison, someone has been regularly paying sums of money into your mother's account.'

'Do you know who it is?'

She shook her head. 'No, I've never known, it was the only secret between myself and Traudi. But if you'd like information about your mother's finances, I know someone who . . .'

'No,' I interrupted her, 'I'm not interested, Frau Freihorst, really.'

She lowered her head: 'But all that she has . . .'

'No,' I repeated, 'let's forget it, please.'

She nodded in resignation.

'Right,' she concluded, spreading her arms, 'I'm going back, I'll leave you alone for a moment.' And she went to join Eva, who had remained in the sitting room.

It was in this room that my mother had slept for years and years. Without ever stirring herself on my behalf. That thought allowed a doubt to slip into my mind: hadn't I perhaps failed in my role as a daughter? Wasn't it my duty to understand, to forgive? I repressed a curious impulse to lie down on my mother's bed. Had I perhaps forgiven her?

To my great surprise, the answer was yes. I *had* forgiven her the hurt she had done to us, to her husband, to her children . . . But as for all the other things she was guilty of, only her victims had the right to condemn or forgive.

Eva appeared in the doorway: 'Are you coming?'

'Come in,' I said.

She walked into the room, instinctively folding her arms over her chest as though to protect herself from an icy draught. Then she looked around, apparently at a loss.

'After all, she's my aunt,' she said with a certain bewilderment.

'That's right,' I replied, 'she's your aunt. I'd never thought of that.'

'I'm curious to see her,' she announced, as though speaking to herself. 'I haven't seen her in a lifetime.'

I had opened the window, and the curtains billowed like sails.

'I feel so sad,' I said.

Eva put an arm around my waist. 'This room is making me sad, too. Come on, let's get back.'

We left. I knew I had set foot in that room for the last time. My mother would never be going back there either.

Frau Freihorst was waiting for us in the sitting room, a true friend whom I doubt my mother really deserved.

We were about to say our goodbyes.

'Can I do anything else for you?' she said.

I thought for a moment.

'I've just got one question,' I replied cautiously, 'but it's a little delicate.'

'Don't worry on my account.'

'All right. In that case I'd like to ask you if you know of the existence of a person, a man, who might, in those days, have been in any way able to influence my mother in her decision to abandon her family.'

She hesitated.

'I don't really know if I should . . .' she began.

'If you don't want to it doesn't matter,' I said hastily.

She bit her lips slightly. She looked like a little girl who has found herself in an awkward situation.

'If you don't want to answer, don't . . .' I broke off with a wave of my hand.

'No, no, I think I can say.' She breathed in, as though taking a run up. 'I don't know if this person is the one you have in mind, but there is a man with whom your mother has never lost contact. He's a former colleague . . .'

'From the . . . SS?'

She nods.

'And is he still alive?'

'Yes, but not in Vienna. In Berlin.'

'Berlin?'

'Yes. He's younger than your mother, he was born in 1915. After the war he was condemned by an Allied court to six years' imprisonment, but he only served three of them. He never married, and lives with a sister who lost her husband and two sons in the war.'

She paused; her eyes were bright.

'They never stopped writing to each other,' she went on after a few moments, 'and since your mother has been here . . . The letters are sent through me. Heinrich . . .'

She smiled as though she had fallen into a trap.

'His name is Heinrich?'

'Yes. And now he sends the letters to my address so that I can pass them on to your mother. But lately she's been taking a long time to answer, and only writes when I'm there with her. No, she's no longer the woman she once was . . .'

She wiped away a tear.

'In the past he came to Vienna a few times . . . I met him. Sometimes I would have dinner with them. I used to feel intimidated by him . . .'

'What did he think about Hitler, after all that time?'

She looked away and locked her fingers together.

'Oh you know, he wouldn't have opened up when I was there . . .'

'Would you give me his address?'

Frau Freihorst hesitated for a moment, then nodded, rummaged in a little box, found a square note pad, tore off a page and scribbled a name and an address on it. I took the sheet of paper, folded it up and put it in my pocket without looking at it.

Time to say our last farewells. But all of a sudden she struck her forehead.

'I nearly forgot!' She went to the bag that she had left on an armchair and, with barely concealed satisfaction and a certain solemnity, she took something out of it.

'Does this remind you of anything?' she asked, holding out a rather battered-looking teddy bear, missing an eye and an ear.

I took it and stared at it, struck dumb with surprise. At first glance it didn't mean anything to me at all, then all of a sudden it came to me.

'I . . . I can't believe it,' I stammered.

'Your mother took it with her that evening, when she abandoned you. She always kept it with her, until she got to Ravensbrück, and there she put it in a strongbox, along with documents, photographs, certificates . . .'

'I can't believe it,' I said again, unnerved.

'It's yours,' she said. 'It's always been yours. When I took it from your mother – and I really had to steal it away from her, believe me – I still didn't know who I was saving it for. But it didn't deserve to end up in the dustbin, among eggshells and banana skins.'

'I don't know what to say,' I murmur. 'I'm touched.'

But there was nothing else to say. It was time to go. I felt worn-out, wearier than I would have expected. I held out my hand to Frau Freihorst, as though to sever the slender bonds that seemed to want to hold me captive. I looked around once more, and felt a lump in my throat. I instinctively gave my mother's friend a quick hug.

'Thank you. Many, many thanks for everything.'

Then Eva and I made our way towards the front door. We had sensed that Frau Freihorst wanted to keep us in the flat a little longer.

We were about to leave when we heard her exclaiming, 'I forgot, he's called Zakopane!'

I turned around. 'Who is?'

'The teddy bear! He's called that because he was bought in Zakopane in Poland.'

I smiled. 'Thank you. Now I remember my grandmother talking about him.'

Eva left first. I followed her, and pulled the door shut behind me.

'Where did you get the teddy bear?' Her tone is acid, her expression threatening.

'If you don't mind I'll leave you alone for an hour or so,' Fräulein Inge says. 'I imagine you'd like to be on your own for a while.'

The guest room is cosy: a television, a wicker bookcase full of books, pretty ornamental plants. I arrange three armchairs beneath one of the three big windows.

'Come on, sit down,' I tell my mother, but she goes

on repeating like a broken record, 'Where did you get that teddy bear? I want to know!'

I walk over to her and hold out my hand: 'Would you give it back to me, please?'

'No!' she snaps, pressing it to her chest. I try to come up with a clever tactic. I open the bag and take out my lipstick.

She stares at it, confused.

'Swap?'

She purses her lips. It seems to me that she's trying to control herself with all her power, because she starts to shake her head vehemently. But soon desire for the lipstick defeats her.

'I've lost mine,' she whines. 'I lost it a long time ago . . . It was in a gold case.'

'Problem solved,' I reply, with an encouraging smile. 'I'll give you the lipstick, and you give me the teddy bear.'

'N-no,' she says hesitantly. But when I make as if to put the lipstick back in the bag, she grabs it from my hand, giving me back the toy. Well, I say to myself with satisfaction, that could have gone worse.

The lipstick disappears into the pocket of her jacket, and she looks at me anxiously. 'Are you staying for a while?'

'Of course,' I answer with surprise. 'Do you want me to stay?'

'Yes,' she says, and a helpless, trembling smile appears on her lips. 'Yes, I really want you to stay.'

'We've still got some time,' I reply, softening slightly. And I add agreeably, 'Come and sit near us, please do.'

She makes herself comfortable, smoothing her

clothes precisely over her thin thighs. For a moment there is silence.

'Why don't you tell me something?' I ask her to break the ice. 'How do you like it here? Have you made any friends?'

She doesn't reply immediately. She emits a long sigh, almost a hoarse sob, and declares darkly, 'Stefan is dead.'

Certainly, my father died a long time ago now, but she announces the fact as though it had happened yesterday. An expression of suffering spreads across her face, but then gradually a cloud of tetchy arrogance settles over her eyes.

'He's better off dead!' she exclaims cynically and resentfully. 'He was a bad man. Yes, he was a bad man!' she says, working herself up. 'He was forever trying to obstruct everything I did. He didn't want me to take an interest in politics; every meeting I went to was a tragedy. He didn't want me to make a career in politics, you know? He demanded that I stay at home and clean and cook and look after the children.'

'Didn't looking after the children strike you as the right thing to do?' I ask, disconcerted.

'My comrades had children too, but their husbands weren't as mean and jealous as mine. I couldn't bear it. I couldn't bear all that jealousy, that obtuseness of his. He refused to understand that I had tasks to perform, specific tasks.'

'What did you have to do?'

'Train the auxiliaries. And I got them to respect me, you can be sure of that! I got them standing in straight lines, all right. Why couldn't my husband look after the little girl every now and again?'

'You had two children,' I remind her. I'm getting used to filling in her gaps.

'Two?' she says, baffled.

'You don't remember your son Peter?'

'Peter?'

Her face grows dark. 'Oh, yes. Peter. But he's dead too. He's been dead for ages.'

Her bright eyes seem to cloud over for a moment. She buries her face in her hands.

'My son is dead and I will never see him again,' she whines through her fingers.

'Peter's still alive,' I tell her. That was unwise; she bursts into floods of tears.

'You mustn't come here and tell me lies! You're hurting me. You're hurting me so much that I'll have to ask for some drops.'

Eva glances at me, perplexed. I nod: fine, I'll try not to push her too hard. But my mother is already taking her hands away from her face, and starting to smooth her hair. There's no getting round it: she throws me every time.

'Do you like the colour of my hair?' she asks innocently. I nod mechanically.

'I was fair as a girl,' she begins, with a melancholy air, 'but I can't go to the hairdresser here. You couldn't come one day and take me to the hairdresser?'

I glance uneasily across at my cousin, who gives me a barely perceptible nod in reply, suggesting that I stay on this track. So I reply in the affirmative, knowing that I'm lying.

'Seriously?' my mother rejoices. 'You promise?'

'Of course,' I reply, a little too loudly.

She looks around as though searching for something.

'Where are my flowers?' she asks eagerly.

'Fräulein Inge took them away.'

'Why?' she protests. 'They're mine!'

'You threw them on the floor.'

She stares at me in disbelief. 'Really?'

'Yes.'

She thinks for a moment, searching for an excuse. 'Perhaps because they weren't yellow roses.'

She brushes the problem aside, and returns to the subject of my father.

'I had to leave him,' she recalls in a colourless voice, 'I had no choice. I was so busy . . . And he used to torment me. My sister-in-law tormented me too, she didn't want me to carry out my duties.'

'What duties?' I ask.

'With the Party. And I'd taken an oath, I couldn't go back on it.'

'You'd taken an oath?'

'As a member of the SS I had to take an oath, that's perfectly normal, isn't it? I had to swear absolute obedience and loyalty until death.'

'Why did you take an oath when you knew you had two children to raise?' I say, knowing that it's risky. All of a sudden she raises her head.

'I wanted to! I wanted to be accepted as a member of the SS, I wanted it more than anything else in the world.'

'Was it more important than your family?'

She nods. 'Yes, but you can't understand. No one can understand nowadays . . .'

It's true. I'm discouraged. I feel powerless.

In any case, she was only one of thousands and thousands of women who had allowed themselves to be swept along by the Nazis' ideological propaganda. Though certainly, not everyone had gone so far as to join Himmler's organisation.

She sees that I'm lost in thought, and asks, 'Are you sad? I don't want that! You mustn't be sad!' She gets to her feet as though to embrace me. I manage to stop her just in time: I couldn't bear it, not now.

'Why don't you tell me about your parents?' I suggest.

She narrows her eyes.

'My parents?' she repeats, disoriented. 'Why should I tell you about my parents?'

'They were my maternal grandparents,' I reply, calmly and firmly.

There is genuine vacancy in her eyes. 'Your maternal grandparents,' she murmurs. She can't find her way out of this one. Finally, to round off, she puffs, 'You didn't miss much.'

'Why do you talk about them like that?'

'They were against me,' she mumbles. 'They voted "no" in the plebiscite, just to spite me.'

'Which plebiscite?'

'For the annexation of Austria!' she says, to refresh my memory. 'My parents didn't want it. They didn't want the Nazis and they didn't want the Führer. And they were always opposed to my membership of the Party. They thought I was degenerate and fanatical. So in the plebiscite they voted "no". Perhaps they thought the Party would expel me, but it didn't. Then, when they found out about Ravensbrück, they told me they were disowning me. Disowning your daughter, can you imagine?'

'Ravensbrück?'

All of a sudden she looks at me cagily, like a suspicious old fox.

'Perhaps you don't know . . .' she says evasively. 'It doesn't matter.'

'I know you were in Ravensbrück,' I reply in a neutral voice. 'Why don't you tell me something about it? I'm interested.'

She tilts her head and gives me a sly smile, then she flutters her eyelashes and tries to avoid the question.

'When you were little I used to call you *Mausi*, do you remember?'

She smiles, her face softer now. 'You were stubborn and disobedient,' she remembers, 'you were clever and rebellious. And you used to like hopping on one leg.'

Again I'm thrown: she can twist me around her little finger. All of a sudden I wonder: did I really live with my mother for four years? With my biological mother, the one who brought me into the world? With a real mother, even if she was too busy to be a mum?

I'd rather bring her back to the subject of Ravensbrück, but she continues obstinately down her own path.

'I want to talk about Berlin,' she insists. 'You remember we were living in a fine apartment in Niederschönhausen? And sometimes I would take you to the park, or to a friend's kitchen garden.'

She half-closes her eyes for a moment. 'But your father was always cross . . .' she recalls. 'He wanted to keep me locked up in the house, like being locked in a cage.'

All of a sudden, with one of those unexpected bursts of energy that I have now learned to recognise, she hurls herself out of the armchair and kneels at my feet. She studies me, eyes bright with tears, burying her chin in my lap.

'My daughter,' she repeats two or three times, sighing emphatically. 'Will you come back tomorrow?'

She grips my hands and starts kissing them furiously. 'Don't leave me alone,' she begs, 'never again!'

I feel excruciatingly embarrassed. And as I go to lift her up, she appears to faint. She closes her eyes and drops lifelessly to her knees. With Eva's help, I manage to put her back in her armchair. I'm about to go into the corridor to call someone, when I hear her chuckling behind me: 'So? Where do you think you're going?' I turn around; she gives me a mocking smile.

'I'm fine,' she sniggers. 'You promised you'd come back. And promises are made to be kept. Are you really going to keep your promise?'

I nod, stunned and bewildered.

'I know you're honest,' she says, trying to flatter me. 'You're my daughter. And my daughter is an honest person.'

I wonder how she knows that. She knows practically nothing about me.

She gives a contented, satisfied smile. She smooths her hair and looks at her nails: white, clear as cellophane, neatly trimmed. She continues to amaze me. What happened? Did she fall ill for a moment, or was she playing a trick on me?

And once again she hurls a series of questions at me: 'Are you coming back tomorrow? Will you bring me an ice cream? And some more flowers?' She seems ecstatic at the prospect of seeing me again, and I feel a momentary sense of guilt.

'I don't know,' I say, trying to evade the issue.

'You promised!' she snaps.

With a desperate gesture, she presses her temples with her finger-tips. 'You promised. You promised!'

That's when it happens. That's the turning-point. Something in the depths of my innards revolts, whispers to me.

'I will come back tomorrow, and I'll bring you more flowers – as long as you tell me about Ravensbrück.'

A blatant piece of blackmail. I catch my cousin's look of disapproval, but ignore it.

'I want yellow roses,' my mother announces in a domineering voice.

'And you shall have them, if you tell me about Ravensbrück.'

She eyes me carefully.

'Why do you want to know about Ravensbrück? There was nothing interesting in Ravensbrück.' Her blue, blue eyes are transparent. Pale and transparent.

Really, mother? Wouldn't you say that the experiments on muscle regeneration or bone transplants were interesting in their way?

'From time to time they would take a piece of muscle from the lower part of the leg of some of the prisoners, to check whether and how the tissue was growing back under the plaster. With other victims, they would amputate a healthy arm, leg or shoulder-blade, and an SS doctor would wrap them up to drive in his car to Professor Gebhardt in Hohenlychen, who would have his doctors, Dr Stumpfegger and Dr Schulze, transplant them into patients from his clinic. The guinea-pigs from the Ravensbrück camp, meanwhile, were killed with lethal injections.'[2]

'I've learned that in many camps, including Ravensbrück, experiments were carried out on human guinea-pigs,' I say in a neutral voice to avoid irritating her. 'I'm sure you must know something about that. It would be interesting to hear your views on the matter.'

I realise that I'm not acting in quite a proper manner, but it's as though a demon somewhere inside me has taken my place.

'How did you know that?' she asks suspiciously. I haven't managed to make my voice entirely anodyne, I'm going to have to be more careful.

'It's in the history books,' I reply carelessly. But she'll have none of it.

'Well if these things are in the public domain, why do you want me to repeat them to you?'

'Because you're a witness,' I reply promptly, with a hint of flattery, 'and historical testimony is precious, whatever its source.'

'Precious . . .' She savours the word as though it were a delicious morsel. 'Do you really mean that?'

[2] Eugen Kogon, *Der SS-Staat. Das System der deutschen Konzentrationslager*, Kindler Verlag, Munich, 1946.

'Yes,' I reply, smiling unctuously. But she is avoiding the subject once again.

'I was nothing more than an irrelevant pawn,' she announces with false modesty, as though openly seeking more blandishments from me.

'Oh, no, I don't believe that for a moment,' I say, contradicting her. 'I'm sure they must have entrusted you with quite difficult tasks in Ravensbrück, tasks that only the best, the strongest and the most efficient guards could have carried out. Am I wrong?'

For a fraction of a second I wonder what's going to happen . . .

She has pulled herself up in her chair, in fact, and I can tell from her expression that my flattery has hit home.

'It was my job to assist the doctors,' she replies quickly, though with a hint of reticence.

I don't give her time to change her mind: 'And what did those doctors do?'

'They cured the prisoners,' she replies vaguely.

'And what were your tasks?' My eyes have caught hers, and won't let go.

'I had to . . . take their temperature.' She's lying, probably guided by some distant instinct, but I keep on at her.

'You just said your task was to assist the doctors!' I remind her impatiently. And immediately I rebuke myself: I've spoken too harshly, she'll get annoyed.

Now she has locked herself away in stubborn silence, she purses her lips and stares at me like a wounded child.

'Well?' I insist; then I try to sweeten my tone: 'What

other tasks did you perform as an assistant, apart from taking the patients' temperatures?'

'Nothing,' she replies irritably.

Gently, now, whispers my demon, apply a little pressure . . .

'Fine,' I say, pretending to give up. 'You don't want to talk and I'm not coming back tomorrow. I'm not coming back to see a mother who has nothing to say to me.'

'I want yellow roses,' she mutters crossly.

'No yellow roses,' I declare while a small voice deep within my conscience rebukes me: she's weak in the head, you're not equally matched, you're playing a cowardly trick.

But some dark force drives me implacably onwards.

'I want you to come back,' she says, giving in. 'And I want yellow roses.'

She begins to sob, then immediately stops again. She wipes her eyes with a hem of her military fabric.

'Then talk,' I insist. 'What else did you have to do as an assistant?'

She swallows, then replies in a strange gurgling voice, 'I had to tie the prisoners to the tables.'

'What for?'

'In 1942 Dr Ernst Grawitz, the doctor who took part in almost all of the experiments carried out by the SS on human guinea-pigs, ordered some prisoners in Ravensbrück concentration camp to be infected with staphylococci or the bacilli of gas gangrene, tetanus and mixed cultures of various pathogenic germs, to experiment on the curative effects of sulfanilamides. The doctor in charge of this project was Professor Karl Gebhardt, professor of orthopaedic surgery at Berlin University and doctor in charge of the Hohenlychen clinic, friend and personal doctor to Himmler. He had the operations carried out by SS doctors Schiedlausky, Rosenthal, Ernst Fischer and Herta Oberheuser, without exercising any real and responsible surveillance over their work.

'The prisoners were infected in the lower part of their legs, while being left in the dark about the real purpose of the interventions to which they were being subjected. Often, as the scars of the few survivors demonstrate, and as witnesses confirm, the flesh was cut to the bone. In many cases, apart from bacterial cultures, fragments of wood or shards of glass were added to the wounds. The legs of the guinea-pigs soon began to suppurate. The victims, who were not given any kind of treatment so that the progress of the condition could be observed, died in terrible pain [. . .] For each series of experiments, repeated at least six times, between six and ten young women were used – usually chosen from among the most attractive.

'Professor Gebhardt only came irregularly to Ravensbrück, to inspect the results and examine the wounds of the "patients" who, tied to the tables in rows, had to spend hours waiting for the arrival of the "Herr Professor".

'Professor Gebhardt referred to the results in May of 1943, in a paper entitled *Special experiments on the effects of sulfanilamides*, on the occasion of the third convention of specialist medical advisers to the Academy of Military Medicine in Berlin, which included, among others, the heads of the Medical Services of the Wehrmacht, and the Luftwaffe, the department of public health and so on, along with directors of university clinics and institutes of medical study and research, Hitler's personal doctor Karl Brandt and a large number of eminent and honoured professors of the German Reich.

'In his paper Professor Gebhardt made no effort to conceal the fact that the experiments had been carried out upon prisoners, and even went so far as explicitly to assume full responsibility for them.

'None of those participating raised any objections.' [3]

'Didn't you feel any compassion for those human guinea pigs?' I ask my mother. As I do so, I realise the pointlessness of my question.

She hesitates for a second, lowers her head and stares at her hands.

Then she raises her eyes and declares with a kind of obtuse arrogance, 'No, I felt no compassion,' and she seems to stumble over the words, 'for "those people", because the operations were being carried out for the good of humanity.'

'Meaning?'

'Are you going to tell me that science doesn't always work for the good of humanity?' she asks emphatically.

[3] *Ibid.*

'Those doctors were nothing but charlatans,' I reply with quiet contempt, 'they were pseudo-medical sadists and pseudo-researchers.'

She gives a start, as though she's just been slapped unfairly for something she hadn't done. Now her eyes are staring at me with glassy, stupefying clarity.

'How foolish you are,' she explodes, 'and how wrong. Our doctors were outstanding professionals, and the results of their experiments were published in all the most authoritative medical journals, both in Germany and abroad!'

She gets her breath back; her cheeks have turned strawberry-red with rage.

'Our researchers were invited to the most prestigious medical conventions in the whole world!' she adds heatedly. 'You know nothing. Nothing!'

And she underlines her statement with a peremptory and impatient wave of her hand.

'And I had no right to feel compassion, my sole duty was to obey. Loyalty and obedience, nothing else. Loyalty is an important virtue, believe me!' Now she is waving a pale and severe finger under my nose.

A pause. She turns to look out of the window, towards the tops of the old plane trees swaying in the misty air.

Then she murmurs, '*Ich habe doch eine Härteaus-bildung erhalten,*' as though talking to herself.

I underwent dehumanisation training: might that be an almost unconscious attempt at self-justification?

Yes, mother, I know; I've read your file. They trained you in order to desensitise you to the atrocities that you would witness at the extermination camps, and only the hardest, the thickest-skinned were destined for those.

That's why you were chosen for Birkenau, the most selective camp of all.

Another silence. I'm feeling hot, and I'm getting more tired by the minute, but the demon within me is driving me onwards.

'So you didn't feel any pity for anyone? Never, not for any of the prisoners in Ravensbrück? Not even for the very old, or the very sick?'

Eva gives me a little nudge with her elbow. What on earth are you doing? it seems to mean. I pay no attention, something inside me is starting to boil with rage.

Ask. Ask again. It may be your last chance.

'It's no fun, talking to my daughter!' my mother explodes, sticking her fingers in her ears. 'I'm not listening to you any more.'

Eva takes the opportunity to whisper to me, 'Why are you torturing her? Can't you see there's no point?'

I don't reply. My mother is darting resentful glances at me. Outside the weather is getting worse. A viscous wind lashes sheets of rain against the windowpanes.

Could it be, I wonder, that this woman has never really experienced an emotion apart from those inculcated in her? Love as well as hate, pity as well as cruelty?

'Once,' I hear her say suddenly.

I gesture to her to take her fingers out of her ears.

'Once what?' I ask, curious.

'Once I felt sorry . . . a bit.'

'What had happened?'

'One day a prisoner was assigned to my block. She

had been a comrade, but then she had moved across to the Resistance, and the Gestapo sent her to the camp. The minute she saw me she spat in my face.'

Instinctively I ask, with some irony, 'Did you have her executed?'

She doesn't need to consider her response. 'I put her in the selection for the brothel.'

'What brothel?'

She seems to rummage around in her memory for a moment, then picks up her thread again.

'Yes, it was in 1943. We'd had instructions to set up brothels in the larger camps, and the first one was to be organised in Buchenwald. One morning we guards were ordered to choose suitable prisoners for the transfer, and I chose her.'

Her face hardens, and a subtle, satisfied smile settles on her lips.

'Shortly afterwards I learned that she had died of a venereal disease,' she adds, and twists her fingers in an unusual manner, while I have the impression that a kind of veil is falling across her eyes. It only lasts a moment.

'At first . . . I felt a kind of sorrow,' she admits, as though confessing to a deplorable weakness, 'but I soon overcame it. I couldn't allow myself that kind of emotion, I mean pity and regret for people who deserved to be in a camp. It never happened again. I was in the Waffen-SS, I was. I couldn't permit myself the sentimentality of ordinary people.'

She had transferred sovereignty over her feelings to the Führer, and she continued to defend the fact.

* * *

How many women, on the other hand, in a Berlin ablaze and thick with the stench of corpses, had the child Helga heard raging against their Führer? They had fought tooth and nail, the women of Berlin, to defend their children, often having given birth to them in air-raid shelters or beneath the arches of the underground. In order to feed their own children they had not hesitated to take up arms and confront the guards of the few grocers' shops that had remained open, the ones that supplied the Wehrmacht or Hitler's entourage. As they fled from Eastern Prussia, with the Red Army at their heels, they had dragged five, six or seven children behind them, tying them one to another with a clothesline so as not to risk losing them. After the war, widowed and with no future in sight, they had gritted their teeth and had liaisons with the men of the victorious powers, preferring the shame of being called whores over the unbearable thought of seeing their own children dying of hunger. I wonder how many of those women still loved the Führer during the battle of Berlin.

During those days we lived in utter chaos. Was there any solidarity? Certainly there was, but there was no sentimentality. Hunger had abolished all rules, all principles. If you had to steal to get hold of a bit of food, then you did: everyone, even the children and the old people.

One evening my brave grandfather-by-marriage risked his life at Anhalt station to steal a sack of dried peas. He shot without hesitation – and he a law-abiding man – at the legs of a man who had come after him. He had violated the *Sperrstunde*, the curfew

72

imposed by the Allies. Anyone found on the streets of Berlin after a certain hour was shot on sight by the intransigent military police.

But the people of Berlin were survivors, which is why, *Sperrstunde* or no, they were forever in search of something, mostly food.

Once the catastrophe was over, the women of Berlin – I can bear witness to them above all – got busy to clear the streets of rubble and console and encourage those returning, drained and exhausted, from Hitler's war.

She has dozed off. She has leaned her head against the back of the armchair and gone to sleep like that, all of a sudden, without having shown any sign of tiredness.

I look at her, my old mother, whom I'm seeing for the second time in half a century, and in spite of it all I can't help feeling an impulse of tenderness.

She sleeps motionlessly, her breath barely perceptible, looking unbearably defenceless and forlorn. A new thought pierces me, followed by an attack of anxiety. One day she will go to sleep like this, silent and vulnerable, never to reawaken, and I will be far away. Perhaps someone will inform me by telegram, by the time she's already underground. I feel a pang. She's still my mother, and when she goes a part of me will go with her. But which part? I can't find an answer to that.

'Look at her, she's like a child,' Eva whispers to me.

'Yes,' I murmur in reply, 'a little shadow.'

'You mustn't torment her,' my cousin adds, 'I don't know what got into you.'

'I don't know either . . . She provokes me somehow.

She irritates me, and at the same time I'm moved by her. I'm so confused . . .'

At that moment my mother wakes up, looks around with frightened eyes, and when she sees me mumbles with relief, 'Ah, you're still here . . .' She yawns. 'What were we talking about?'

I avoid reminding her about the inmate she sent to the brothel in Buchenwald, and say, 'Why don't you tell me something about yourself? How do you spend your days, for example?'

She runs a hand over her forehead.

'I stopped doing it in Birkenau,' she announces, as though to justify herself for something she mentioned earlier.

'Stopped doing what in Birkenau?' I can't help asking, despite my good intentions a moment before.

'Tying women to tables.'

She angles her head, but I have time to see her eyes: are they really misted with tears – or is it just my determination to grasp at the merest hint of regret?

She leans forward once again and grips my hands before I can do anything to stop her.

'You mustn't think I was acting on my own initiative,' she says quickly, revealing a hint of concern. Her hands, so cold and bony, fill me with a sense of unease.

'What are you talking about?' Her proximity disturbs me. I free myself from her grip with an almost hysterical gesture. I feel relieved, while she stares at her hands as though someone had just taken away something she was holding.

'I'm talking . . . about Birkenau,' she replies, slowly and uncertainly.

'You said you weren't acting on your own initiative,' I suggest.

'Oh, yes! That's it . . . I mean . . . the fact that I treated them strictly.'

'Who?'

'The prisoners on my block. I couldn't treat them with kid gloves, could I?' She smiles, in search of agreement.

I nod mechanically.

'I had orders to treat them with extreme harshness,' she crows, 'and I made them spit blood.'

The mask she was wearing a moment before slips from her face, all concern vanishes.

'I'm talking about those idlers who worked in the munitions factories, you know the ones? They were always tired and difficult, and at night they whined for the children they had lost along the way.'

She adds with enthusiasm: 'I put a rocket under them!' And she immediately continues as though explaining a technical term: 'It's military slang. That's what they used to say. Putting a rocket under someone meant working them to death.'

She stares at me: her expression as it was before.

'They needed discipline, you know? Those Jewish whores had to understand where they were and above all why. And there was only one way of doing that: discipline, harsh and inflexible discipline. That's the secret if you want to maintain control of a camp.'

I look at you, mother, and I feel a terrible, lacerating rift within me – between the instinctive attraction for my own blood and the irrevocable rejection of what you have been, of what you still are.

* * *

That's enough, I tell myself, you've come here to see her one last time, to try and ensure that it ends well. I try to smile at her, but my lips are set in a rigid grimace, hard as concrete. The demon returns to drive me onwards. Why not give in to it?

What was the food like for the guards in Birkenau?

While she was acting the incorruptible SS woman, my brother and I were suffering from the most terrible hunger. After 1944, food supplies for the ordinary German population had dried up almost entirely. They ate bread made with rape seed, they ground tree bark and acorns to make flour – which gave you a terrible stomachache – or gulped down revolting soups made of nettles.

'Were you short of food?' I ask. Eva casts me a disappointed glance, and my mother cackles. The question seems to amuse her.

'We had everything,' she boasts, 'the comrades made sure we wanted for nothing: real coffee, salami, butter, Polish vodka, cigarettes, scented soap. We had silk stockings and real Champagne, although only at Christmas.'

Your comrades, mother. After more than half a century, you still talk of them with such a sense of solidarity, with such undying deference.

'I was an absolute bookworm, for example' she continues animatedly, 'and the comrades, when they came back from Berlin, always brought me something interesting to read.' She draws herself up proudly. 'I wasn't one of those who only read popular news-papers like some of my comrades. No, I read impor-tant books, you know? And that reading helped me to relax before going to sleep. After all, I was a human being, wasn't I?'

I can't contain myself: 'How could you go to sleep knowing that thousands of corpses were burning only a few yards away?'

I don't need to look at Eva to feel her sad eyes upon me. But it's done now.

My mother, in turn, replies almost contemptuously.

'I never suffered from insomnia in Birkenau. And anyway, I've already told you, I'd been strictly trained. I couldn't permit myself to . . .' But then a strange thing happens: her jaw begins to tremble. It's a grotesque, piteous spectacle.

She presses her lips together tightly in an attempt to stop the trembling, but rather than diminishing it grows; it becomes uncontrollable, it alters her features. Now her face is both helpless and contorted with rage.

'The ones who were burned were just scum,' she announces contemptuously. 'Germany had to get rid of every last *Stück*, every last member of that wretched race.'

'And did you support that?'

'What? Did I support the Final Solution? Why do you think I was there? For a holiday?'

She laughs, but her jaw is still trembling.

'Didn't you even feel sorry for the children?' I ask. I don't dare meet Eva's eye.

'And why should I have?' she replies promptly. 'A Jewish child would have become a Jewish adult, and Germany had to free itself of that loathsome race, how many times do I have to repeat that?'

I take a deep breath.

'But you were a mother,' I object, 'you had two children. While the children were being driven into the gas chambers, didn't you ever think about us?'

'What's that got to do with it?'

'I mean . . . didn't it ever occur to you that if we'd been Jewish children we'd have faced the same fate?'

'My children were Aryan!' she exclaims, outraged. 'The Aryans had nothing to fear. My children were perfect, and no one would have touched a hair on their heads!'

Are you really sure about that, mother? Do you really think that we Aryan children had a comfortable place in Hitler's greater Germany? When, for example, in February 1943, Minister of Propaganda Josef Goebbels announced the imposition of severe emergency restrictions, do you think that Aryan children would have been exempted?

As for not touching a hair on our heads, fine. They didn't send us into the gas chambers, but they did starve us most appallingly: at night we dreamed of potatoes. And I had to confront all that without you. Because you weren't there. You had delegated your role as a mother to others so that you could follow your own path.

Even in 1971, when I came to see you in Vienna with my son, not for a minute did you try to recover the time we had lost, or re-establish any kind of relationship with me; you just tried to get me to wear your SS uniform.

And today, once again, I haven't had so much as a spark of genuine maternal warmth from you.

I look at you, and I remember the slender diary that

my paternal grandmother gave me shortly before she died. My father had placed it in her hands, and she wanted to give it to me. From those pages I understood that Papa had never forgotten you, even though you had broken his heart. He had never forgotten you, in spite of pretty young Ursula, the girl 'of good family' whom he had married the second time around.

And I have never managed to erase you from my life either.

'No one would have touched a hair on your heads.' We're still on that topic.

'During the war, didn't you ever wonder what had become of your children?' I've had that question inside me for so long. As I ask it, I notice with relief that her jaw is no longer trembling.

She looks at me vacantly.

'The war . . .' she repeats dreamily. 'In Birkenau I didn't even notice it. I had so many things to do . . .'

She pushes back her hair.

'But then the Russians came.' Her face becomes animated again. 'It was in January . . . Yes, it was cold.'

The memory comes into focus. 'The Russians arrived and treated us like criminals.' Her voice is stung with outrage. 'They threatened us with guns and forced us to take off our uniform jackets.'

She automatically makes the gesture of taking off her jacket.

'They wanted to see the inside of our arms,' she goes on, 'to check if we had tattoos showing our blood group.'

Her teeth squeak strangely as she laughs.

'But the SS women didn't have the tattoo, you see?' She pulls back the sleeve of her jacket and reveals her arm. 'You see, no tattoo.' What I see is her wrinkled and alarmingly white skin.

'But we put on the uniform,' she repeats, growing more and more tearful, more and more senile. 'We guards had SS uniforms. One comrade tried to be clever, and said to the Russians, pointing at her uniform, "*Odolzhat! Odolzhat!*" She wanted them to think she'd borrowed it. But the Russians beat her, shouting "*Lguna!*" Liar, that's what they said.'

She wipes away a tear. 'We were separated, men from women. We were sad. The men shouted "*Heil Hitler!*" from their truck, and the Russians beat them with their rifle butts, but some of them shouted "*Heil Hitler!*" anyway, putting their lives at risk.'

I'm distracted. My thoughts return to the victims, to all the stories I know, the stories I've read or been told. I also think, mother, that it's only by hating you that I could finally tear myself away from you. But I can't. I can't get that far.

I've got to get back to her. She's noticed my detachment, and she's demanding attention.

'Why have you stopped talking?' she asks sulkily.

I feel tired and disappointed. By now I'm close to resignation. She's gone; I've seen her for the last time. I can start to bring this meeting to an end. I look at the clock.

'I still have so many questions to ask you,' I say prudently, 'but I can see it's getting late. Soon you'll have to go to lunch and we . . .'

'Ask, ask away,' she says quickly, with a hint of anxiety.

'Let's talk about your health,' I suggest. 'What do they do to you here? Do they give you any kind of treatment?'

'Just ask about Birkenau,' she pleads. 'Because that's what you're interested in, isn't it?'

Her expression is knowing and alert once again. Another of those astonishingly sudden changes of hers.

Nonetheless, I try to keep to the direction I've set myself.

'Talk to me about you,' I insist. 'So, do they give you any treatment? What do they give you?'

She cuts me short. 'I imagine Fräulein Inge will already have told you what they give me. Pills and syrups, that's what. And I'm not actually convinced that they do any good. They want to improve my memory, but what good is it to me?' And she adds astutely, 'Everything I want to remember I always find in the usual place, and the rest doesn't interest me.'

There's a moment of silence, and then she gives me an encouraging smile. 'So? Don't you want to know more about Birkenau?'

Now that she's pressing me, I realise that I've run out of questions. But I do feel a faint sense of anxiety at the thought of our imminent separation.

'What are you thinking about?' she asks solicitously, almost sweetly. She leans forwards and grips my hands again.

But I don't want to make her the gift of my confusion, and I fall back on one of those stories that have recently crowded into my mind. It was told to me by the protagonist himself.

'I was thinking about someone I know . . .'

'Who?' This time she's the one who looks me straight in the eyes, and I'm forced to avert my gaze.

'A friend,' I reply.

'Why were you thinking about him?'

'He was deported to Auschwitz at the age of eighteen, he was castrated.' And I quickly free my hands from hers.

She draws back with a puff of irritation. 'Castrated in Auschwitz?' she asks, scornful and incredulous. 'He's been telling you a pack of lies.'

This time I explode: 'They exposed his reproductive organs to X-rays for twenty minutes, giving him very severe burns, and then they removed his testicles to dissect them and examine them under a microscope. Are you going to deny that they experimented with the sterilisation of human beings in Auschwitz?'

'It's a lie!' she insists. And clarifies: 'Some things were only done in Ravensbrück.'

'And what about Mengele?' I remind her. 'Doesn't that name mean anything to you?'

'Mengele?' she echoes, as though shifting the word from one side of her mouth to the other. 'Never heard of him.'

I feel as if I'm being provoked, played for a fool.

'And Meyer, Kaschub, Langben, Heyde, Renno, Brandt – do those names mean nothing either?'

Her mouth is thin and hard. 'Never heard of them, I don't know who you're talking about.'

She frowns and folds her arms. 'And anyway I don't want to talk to you any more, you've annoyed me now.'

She gets to her feet, apparently in a terrible mood all of a sudden. She takes a few steps through the room: she walks upright, apparently quite steady on her feet. She walks over to an ornamental plant and starts picking off red berries and popping them slowly between her fingers.

'Say something nice to her,' Eva hisses to me, 'you must leave her in a balanced state of mind.'

She's right. But while I'm searching for something conciliatory to say, I hear her muttering, 'You've never once called me *Mutti*.' She wipes her hands with a handkerchief and repeats, 'You say you're my daughter and you've never once called me *Mutti*!'

She comes over to me and asks in a hurt and doleful voice, 'Am I not your mother?' And with a certain mischief she starts pinching my cheek as though I were a little girl. I nod mechanically, and she starts shrieking, 'Then you have to call me *Mutti*! Everyone else's children call their mothers *Mutti*, and you have to call me *Mutti* too. I want you to.'

She crosses her arms over her chest and assumes a domineering expression. I feel helpless, caught off guard. I can't call her *Mutti*. I can't do it.

'I'm waiting,' she insists, in the intransigent voice of someone who is sure of their rights. I could reply that everyone else's children have probably had a lifetime to get used to calling their mothers *Mutti*, but I'm afraid of annoying her.

'I can't say it,' I decide to admit.

'You can't call me *Mutti*?' she scoffs.

'I'm not used to it,' I answer, shrugging my shoulders.

'I want you to call your mother *Mutti*!' she insists. It comes across as capricious, nothing more than that. 'If you don't I'm going to leave here and I'm not even going to come back to say goodbye to you,' she says vindictively, in a defiant tone.

'I can't do it,' I say curtly, irritated and dismayed. But she starts playing a new role. She hides her face in her hands and starts snivelling.

'I don't understand why you came here to humiliate me . . . To humiliate an old mother who asks only to be called *Mutti*.' And she weeps and sobs and coughs: we're back in the world of melodrama. My inner demon starts to goad me again.

Blackmail her, it suggests to me. Tell her you'll only call her *Mutti* if she's more open with you.

There's no way out.

'Perhaps your friends' children call their mothers *Mutti* because there are no lies between them.' I listen to my voice and don't recognise it: it sounds like someone else's voice.

'I never tell lies!' insists my mother, resentfully.

'That's not true,' I contradict her. 'You said you'd never heard Mengele's name mentioned before.'

She gives a twisted smile. 'Well, maybe I forgot.'

'Fine,' I answer slyly, 'but that's enough. Stop telling lies. It's absurd to have lies between a mother and daughter, don't you think?'

She falls silent and stares at me with the candour of a child. She nods. Finally a sly little smile flickers across her face.

'If I tell you the truth will you call me *Mutti*?'

I smile to myself.

'Fine,' I reply. And without delay I return to the subject closest to my heart.

'I told you about that friend of mine who was castrated in Auschwitz . . .'

She lowers her eyes and shakes her head.

'Did you know they were doing . . . those things in Auschwitz?'

I hear my cousin sigh, but once again I pay no attention.

'Of course!' my mother erupts impatiently. 'Of course I knew, I was in the Waffen-SS, and we all knew what was going on.'

'Did you personally know any of those doctors in Auschwitz who performed sterilisation exp –'

'Brack,' she interrupts. 'I knew Dr Brack quite well.'

There, I think to myself: at last.

'Really? And did you ever talk about what he was doing . . . for the good of humanity?' I ask, using her own words.

'Yes,' she agrees, 'once. There was a party . . . a wedding, in fact. A colleague of mine had got married to an SS comrade. We were celebrating that . . . and he, Brack, was a bit over-excited, and then . . .'

She fixes me with a sly look. 'First you have to call me *Mutti*, and then I'll tell you what Brack said.'

'Fine,' I give in, but it takes a great effort to frame the word '*Mutti*'.

My mother stares at me: she's waiting. Why is this so important after half a century? It can't be anything but a senile whim, she wants to be on a par with her companions.

Mutti . . . But she doesn't deserve it. She's never

shown the slightest trace of maternal love, and she's sitting there stiffly, arrogantly, waiting arrogantly for my '*Mutti*' – her trophy. But I remember our pact, and what I stand to get in return.

I make a huge effort. '*Mutti*,' I manage to say.

She rejoices, clapping her hands. 'Again, again!'

'*Mutti*.'

Then she subsides into floods of tears – too high-pitched, too shrill. Perhaps she realises; she realises she can't move me to tears. Then she calms down, settles back into her armchair, arranges her face into a stubborn mask and mutters, 'I don't want to talk about that horrible man Brack. And anyway there were things he didn't talk about. He didn't talk about what he was doing in the scientific experiment block . . . It was a secret, you know? A state secret.'

Lying, opportunistic, fanatical, disloyal: that is how her file describes her.

In his book *Der SS-Staat*, Eugen Kogon includes a report from SS Oberführer Victor Brack addressed to Heinrich Himmler, about the preliminary experiments into the sterilisation of human beings:

'The following result may be considered secure and scientifically founded:

With a view to the permanent sterilisation of individuals, it is possible to apply doses of X-rays high enough to produce a castration with all the related consequences. The high dose of X-rays destroys the internal secretion of the ovaries or testicles [. . .] But as it is not possible to screen the surrounding tissue with lead, we must accept the inconvenient fact that these organs will be damaged, with the consequent apparition of so-called "after-effects" of the X-rays. In case of excessive intensity of radiation, over the following days or weeks burns will appear on the areas of skin affected by the rays.'

Because the intention was to proceed with the sterilisation of the subjects without their knowledge, Dr Brack made a suggestion:

'One practical method might, for example, be to summon the individuals to a counter in front of which they would have to remain for about three minutes to answer questions or fill in forms. The clerk behind the counter would be able to switch on the radiological apparatus in such a way as to activate both the X-ray tubes, given that the radiation has to come from both sides. In this way, with a dual-tube apparatus, it would be possible to sterilise between 150 and 200 people a day, and with 20 such sets of between 3,000 and 4,000. [. . .] The fact that those affected will discover, after a period of weeks or months, that they have become sterile is of no importance.

If you, Reichsführer, were to opt for this solution, in the interests of maintaining the equipment, Reichsleiter Bouler would be willing to place at your disposal all the staff and doctors necessary for the implementation of the project.'

* * *

'Now you're angry,' my mother observes. She tilts her head and gives me a rueful smile.

'And anyway I didn't know that man Brack very well,' she admits weakly.

She has deceived me and she knows it. I feel cold inside.

'When you were little you were so pretty,' she says, trying to get around me, 'so pretty that my friends insisted that I have your photograph published in a race journal.'

Her friends . . . I struggle to concentrate again.

'What year are you referring to?'

'What year?' she repeats. She makes a gesture as though to wave a wisp of fog away from her eyes.

'Were you still . . . with Papa?' I ask cautiously.

'With Stefan?' She shrugs.

At any rate, those 'friends' must have been hers alone. And all of a sudden a vivid memory returns.

A summer-house in Kremmen, a little village not far from Berlin. Stone foundations, the rest built of wood. Summer furniture: wicker and pale pine.

The windows are open; from the village square, lined with old horse chestnuts, comes the sound of bells.

You reach the house through a little front garden, but everything happens at the rear of the house. In the courtyard, among the lime trees, the neighbours' goose beats its wings as it runs after my brother Peter, trying to peck him.

A little gate made of twisted interlocking planks leads into a garden whose colours, sounds and perfumes I can still clearly remember: the jasmines, the elders, whose berries could be used to make a strange wine-coloured soup, the dog roses that made a fine, sweet jam.

And the cheerful song of the larks, the swallows under the eaves and two storks on the roof of a nearby barn. I still hadn't realised that we were at war.

The scene takes place in the sitting room. It is evening, the sun is still low; the soil in the garden gives off a damp, pleasant odour.

We have guests. My mother is laughing a lot. Apart from her I remember another woman and three men. The guests are all in uniform, including the woman.

Then my mother picks up Peter, who is kicking his legs and squealing. She wants him to give each of the guests a kiss on the cheek, but he begs to differ. Each time she brings him to a guest, he tosses his curly head in another direction. He's being naughty, and has no intention of kissing strangers.

My mother starts to get cross, and her voice hardens. 'Little nuisance!' But he's fed up, and delivers a punch to the stomach of a uniformed man rather than kiss his sandpapery cheek. The recipient lets out a little shriek of amusement. My mother, disappointed, puts the little rebel back on the ground, whereupon he starts crawling on his hands and knees through the sitting room making funny, childish sounds. I see him as though he were right before me, blithe and lively.

I don't see any good coming of this and try to sneak off, but my mother catches me. It's my turn. The same bit of play-acting. I feel a cramp in my stomach. I don't like kissing strangers either. But she has her eagle eye on me, and I resign myself to distributing my kisses, however reluctantly. But then I come to a man I dislike.

I have disliked him since the moment I first saw him. He is tall and has scary eyes. His eyes are very pale, like Siamese cats' eyes. They seem to emit shards of glass.

Here I am in front of him. The man bends down, gives me an icy smile, and stretches forward to receive that stupid kiss. But it's too much for me – I bite him on the chin.

He starts back, clutching his chin. Yelling, my mother grabs me and shakes me. I don't cry, but I hate everyone.

A quarter of an hour later. There's no one left in the sitting room. Peter has found the dustpan, and is cheerfully stamping on it. Then he sits down on it as though it were a sledge. I squat on the ground and watch him. He's a real little devil.

All of a sudden someone throws a big fishing net over us. I didn't know there was one in the house, and I don't understand why it's been thrown over us, but I'm terribly frightened.

I scream, and Peter screams too, he clutches me and yells at the top of his voice. We clumsily scrabble about, but the more we try to free ourselves from the net's embrace, the more entangled we become, the more we shriek.

There is no sign of the grown-ups. Perhaps they are spying from behind the door, enjoying our pathetic anxiety, our forlorn terror.

We're like two beetles on their backs. We wave our legs around and scream. The sun has set and the shadows of evening are coming in through the window.

A trap. A trap set by a world of adults, suddenly cynical and malevolent.

(My mother had frightened us on other occasions, above all when she handed out her implacable punishments. If my stepmother's motto was 'Don't think, know', my mother's was 'Above all, obey'. She was hypersensitive to disobedience. She couldn't bear the slightest hint of insubordination. Every time – being rebellious by nature – I showed the slightest sign of insurrection, she would punish me by locking me in the shed. In Berlin, when we were living in the district of Niederschönhausen, we had one that had only a tiny little window, but my mother had covered it over with cardboard so that I would stay in total darkness for hours. Another punishment that I considered particularly terrible when I was about four years old was the administering of a triple ration of cod liver oil. Peter, who still became absolutely terrified when he felt our mother growing more nervous and agitated than usual, feared that special spoon as though it were the devil incarnate, and the minute he saw it he started to shriek in desperation. One day he refused the spoon so firmly that the oil splashed in my mother's face. She was incandescent with fury and locked him up – after also giving him the punitive ration of cod liver oil – in the big wardrobe in our parents' room (by this time my father had already been called up). Once in there, my brother was in danger of suffocating: when she let him out he was lying on the bottom, his head lolling on a shoebox. That gave my mother a genuine scare, and she started to shake little Peter. He looked as though he was dead or unconscious, though he was probably only woozy with the lack of oxygen.)

The Kremmen nightmare continues. There is no sign

of the adults, and Peter and I are still imprisoned in that horrible fishing net. Peter is making a terrible noise, clinging on to me and digging his nails into my arms. It is as though reality has been turned on its head. We feel as though we have been catapulted into a dark and unknown world, in which our mother has suddenly become a witch in order to amuse her friends with a cruel and stupid prank.

I start calling out to my mother in a high and pleading voice, '*Mutti! Mutti!*' I shout, sobbing and begging her to come and let us out. Finally she comes. She laughs until the tears come to her eyes. Her guests laugh too. They have clearly been amusing themselves. And I, caught somewhere between relief and rancour, hate them all even more, but above all I hate the man I bit, who is now laughing uncontrollably, showing his long, pointed teeth, and looking like a big fat shark.

It's over; our mother releases us.

Since that day both my brother and I have suffered from claustrophobia.

Peter was born in Berlin, in that flat in Nordendstrasse, in the district of Niederschönhausen.

When, a few years later, our stepmother entered our lives, my brother immediately accepted her, instinctively and without reservation. For about a year after our mother had gone, our grandmother had looked after us, and by the time my father married Ursula, Peter seemed to have forgotten his biological mother completely. Our stepmother gave me instructions to tell him that she was not his real mother; I promised, and

I kept my word. We came up with the notion that Ursula had been ill for a long time, and that she had finally come home from a hospital far away, and Peter remained utterly convinced that she was his real mother. I said nothing, at first because I was afraid of my stepmother, and then because deceit becomes a habit over time.

But it's not enough.

One morning immediately after the war was over, when everything was chaos, destruction and loss, and no one was able to tell the new authorities anything at all on the grounds that they had lost their documents – and many people really had lost them after the bombing raids that had levelled houses, offices and archives – our stepmother went to certify the birth of my brother, declaring him to be her biological son. This lie was maintained over the years, until Peter began to get together the documents for his marriage, at which point the Austrian authorities (we had returned to Vienna in 1948) asked to see his real birth certificate, and he called it up from the state registry in Berlin. The reply came promptly, and in the space marked 'mother's name', he read a surname and a Christian name that he had never seen before in his life.

His beloved 'mother' had been deceiving him for twenty-six years, with the complicity of my father and my stepmother. Even our paternal grandmother had been involved: every time she talked to us about my father's first wife she seemed to imply that I was 'that witch's' only child. So Peter had lost not just one mother, but two. This belated revelation traumatised him deeply, and created a great gulf between him and our stepmother.

Grandmother told me that my mother refused to celebrate Christmas according to the Christian tradition. Such was her blind loyalty to the SS that she stopped going to church, and on 24 December she celebrated the *Sonnenwendfest*, a festival inaugurated on Himmler's orders. The SS distributed booklets containing instructions as to how and when the festivities should be celebrated.

For example, my grandmother said that at Christmas my mother went to a great deal of trouble to make biscuits in the shape of a particular rune which the SS saw as signifying the eternity of the world, a garland which signified eternal return, and a snail, representing the sun from which life on earth arose. Those sweets were to be the only decorations on the spruce tree, because the booklet forbade everything else – silver tinsel, coloured straws and the various sentimental knickknacks that the Germans have always liked to hang on their Christmas trees.

Grandmother, who came with grandfather from Poland at Christmas to bring presents for me and Peter, violently disagreed with my mother, saying that her 'SS hobby horses' shouldn't be allowed to deprive us children of a traditional festival which was celebrated by all 'normal people'. There were furious arguments, and once grandmother managed to throw all the biscuits my mother had made into the bin. They almost came to blows. My grandparents quickly returned to Poland.

Later my father, who also disapproved of his wife's

political activism, would always defend her to his mother, to the latter's fury; from the first, Grandmother had been hostile to 'that madwoman' whom her son had insisted on leading to the altar whatever the cost.

As for my mother's fanaticism, I think it was typical of the double morality of the SS: an outwardly austere façade of rigour, pride, moderation and temperance masked great gulfs of excess, fanaticism and conceit – and a limitless thirst for power.

Fräulein Inge appears at the door. 'How are we doing? Can I get you ladies anything? Tea, coffee or anything else?' Behind her, someone peers curiously into the guest room.

My mother protests disagreeably: 'You never offer *me* anything at this time of day.'

Fräulein Inge comes into the room.

'But today is a special day! Your guests have come from so far away . . .'

My mother glances at me in surprise. 'Far away? Where have you come from?'

'Italy,' I reply.

'Why Italy?'

'Because that's where I live.'

'Since when?'

'Since 1963.'

She's perplexed. 'In Italy . . .' she repeats several times. 'My daughter lives in Italy.'

Fräulein inquires politely, 'So, ladies, what can I bring you?'

Before Eva and I can reply, my mother declares imperiously, 'I want an apple juice!'

Fräulein Inge nods. 'Fine. And the ladies?'

Eva asks for a coffee, and I do too, although I know it won't be the way I like it.

Once Fräulein Inge has left, my mother sits in silence for a few moments. She has gone to sit by one of the big windows, far away from me, and she looks as though she's seeking refuge. From there, with a gloomy expression on her face, she shrieks, 'I don't want to be interrogated! You've come here from Italy to interrogate me, and I'm not having it!'

I'm dismayed: is she hurling a truth at me, and I just can't see it?

'I have no intention of interrogating you,' I say, trying to reassure her. But she crouches in her armchair and, body stiff and eyes narrowed, croaks in a voice that seems to come from beyond the grave, 'I am innocent. I am not guilty. I obeyed orders, like everyone else. Everyone obeyed orders. All of my comrades, and all the Germans, what's the point of denying it? Even children blindly obeyed their teachers, following orders from above.'

She waves a trembling finger at me.

'You obeyed too!' she snarls venomously. 'In school they taught you to hate the Jews and you hated the Jews. Try telling me that's not true!'

Her eyes are flashing scornfully, her whole attitude is menacing. In all the time I've been here I've never seen her so overexcited and resentful.

'You came from Italy to put me on trial, but now I'm going to turn the tables on you!' she shrieks, her voice quivering with malice. 'I'm not going to let you interrogate me, do you hear! I won't let you do it!'

She's breathing with difficulty, ashen-faced, flaming patches of red above her cheekbones.

'Everyone spits on Germany now,' she says furiously, 'and do you know why? Because we lost the war. If we had won, the whole world would have kissed the Führer's feet, not just his feet.'

She cackles. 'Not just his feet,' she repeats, pleased with her joke.

They are old words, words that I have heard uttered many times, after the war, by the survivors in Berlin. After the capitulation of 1945, crushed by the international chorus of hatred and contempt, many Germans had imagined that they could reacquire a scrap of pride by saying such things.

I exchange a glance with Eva, but my mother is already repeating the malign accusations she voiced a few moments ago: 'You can't get away from me, my dear, don't act the innocent! Can you claim in all honesty that you have never felt hatred towards a Jew?'

I find myself hoping that Fräulein Inge is going to come back in with the coffee, but she doesn't. 'Just you think about it!' croaks my mother's voice in a falsetto.

She has won. An unpleasant memory creeps back into my reluctant mind.

In 1943 I had been sent to boarding school in Eden, in the suburb of Oranienburg. The pupils lived in a solidly built house with dormitories in the attic, gardens and orchards. But the foul breath of the war, filled with violence and death, reached even this little Eden.

I hated being sent away from Berlin, from my

brother and my new grandfather who loved me. It was, as I have said, my stepmother who sent me into exile.

But I had found understanding and affection at that boarding school. I had learned to love the headmistress, Frau Heinze – the only person, I repeat, whom I ever, once I was abandoned by my mother, called *Mutti*.

The inmates of the boarding school were children who had been rejected by their families for various reasons – often, as in my case, mere excuses. The children of failed marriages or divorced parents, orphans, or children rejected by parents unwilling to have them in the house.

And the war took care of the rest.

The sound of enemy gunfire reached us from a long way off, but at night it terrified us. At the beginning of the war, I was told, only soldiers died, but soon it would be the turn of the civilian population. The soldiers didn't die, they 'fell', and monuments were erected in their honour. Civilians didn't fall, they died, and no one thought of erecting monuments to their memory, or in memory of their children, wives, mothers.

Once our nocturnal fears had been overcome, we had slides and swings and see-saws to entertain us during the day, and as we pushed ourselves high up into the air, as we looked beyond the school grounds we could see the country road, flanked with plane trees, where the soldiers marched between a haycart on one side and a dung barrel on the other, or the armoured cars of the Wehrmacht rumbled along on their caterpillar tracks, making the earth shake.

In the evening, when Mamma Heinze handed out the meagre bread rations, I always managed to get a smile from her, sometimes even a caress. These were new and precious sensations for me: they cheered me, and they were a powerful source of strength.

One morning as we left our dormitories the frost was on the ground. The school was no more than three hundred yards away and we went there on our own, a flock of little sheep with the older children, of eleven or twelve, at its head. We called ourselves '*Mutti* Heinze's children'. We felt a strong sense of solidarity.

About fifty yards from the school building we noticed a crowd of people furiously beating somebody. As we approached we saw that their victims were a man and a woman. We stood there, frightened and alarmed, as we watched that blind violence, until one boy broke away from the gang of brutes and told us that they were a Jewish couple. They had lived in hiding for a while, protected by a family friend, but then he had been called up and, after surviving for a few weeks with practically nothing to eat, they had been forced out into the open.

The head of our little flock said, 'Let's go to school.'

One little girl burst into tears. 'Why are they beating those people?' Meanwhile the poor couple, bruised and bleeding and in a wretched state, pleaded with their attackers not to hand them over to the Gestapo.

All of a sudden one of their assailants called out to us, 'Come on, kids, if you're good National Socialists, give us a hand!' His comrades echoed his words in a chorus of encouragement.

I can't say exactly how it happened. All I know is

that something like an electric charge ran through us all, as though some kind of primordial aggression, or some kind of contagious hatred had been awoken within us.

We hurled ourselves en masse on the two unfortunates, kicking and punching. Some of us spat on them, others stamped on the hands of the two unarmed victims as they lay there on the beaten earth. I leaned over the woman and pulled her hair. I pulled hard and shouted, 'Bloody Jew!' She looked at me in fear and dismay. I will never forget that look.

The poor woman's head was in a cowpat that had encrusted in her hair, but I felt neither compassion nor pity for her.

Someone, of course, had alerted the Gestapo, and they arrived with a truck which looked enormous to me; it would have held not just two Jews, but fifty. Shouting hysterically, five or six SS men jumped out, along with a team of snarling dogs.

Just as I'm admitting to myself that I'm in no position to cast the first stone, Fräulein Inge comes in with the two coffees and the apple juice.

My mother pounces eagerly on her glass, draining it in one gulp. Then she puts it on the table and stares at me uncertainly.

'Where were we?'

I'm hoping she's lost the thread, but she declares confidently, 'You're not a bit like your father, you're just like me.'

She's right, I think regretfully. I so wanted to be like my father, and instead my brother was the one who inherited his features, while I am the image of my mother.

The last words we exchanged before Fräulein Inge arrived must have slipped her mind, and yet what she says next in a sense brings us back to where we were before.

'Even your father bowed to the regime,' she says with a hint of malign irony, 'and him so pure, so filled with noble ideals. He was a gifted man, a fine painter. Just think, when I knew him he was spending his time with people like Schlichter, Grosz, Klee, Dix, Nolde . . .'

She glances at me as though dubious of my knowledge of art history. 'But perhaps those names mean nothing to you,' she concludes.

I let it pass, because apart from anything she's moved on.

'Stefan devoted himself to the neoclassicism that the Führer demanded,' she clearly recalls. 'He started painting landscapes and portraits, sunsets and still lifes, peasants and tractors, people at work, horses and country scenes . . . He also copied out exotic animals from natural history books. He held exhibitions. It was at one of those exhibitions that he met Hilde, who bought a painting from him: "Lions in the Savannah".'

She smiles mischievously. 'And once I was gone good old Hilde wasted no time, and introduced her little sister to Stefan.'

I'm surprised, I didn't know about any of this.

'A nasty piece of work, she was,' my mother announces bitterly. 'I never liked Hilde. I expect she thought she was really something because she worked for the Ministry of Propaganda, and I'm still thoroughly convinced that she was infatuated with Goebbels, but of course he barely noticed she was there. She was very efficient, I wouldn't deny that for a second, but Goebbels didn't pay any attention to her as a woman . . . He had all those actresses at his feet, and then he had that affair with Baarova . . . No, Goebbels just saw her as a capable and trustworthy secretary.'

I watch her with growing amazement. She can change from one moment to the next, like a chameleon.

She isn't wearing any jewels, not even a ring. Nothing. Her nails and hair are neat and tidy. She seems still to have some connection with the rigour and the military discipline of the past.

I'm interested in what she has to say about my aunt by marriage. I remember a cold and distant Hilde in Berlin in the '40s. She always hurried home to change, and then she would immediately return to the office. As the war got worse, we saw her less and less often: often she would sleep in the ministry bunker, or in Goebbels's private bunker in his villa overlooking the Tiergarten. At that time all I knew was that she was working for that man whose voice came bellowing from the loudspeakers in the street or from our radios at home; it was only much later that I really understood who Josef Goebbels was, and what position he occupied in the Reich hierarchy.

My mother falls silent, having piqued my curiosity. I ask her another question about Hilde, but all of a sudden she flies into a rage: 'Your father didn't wait so much as a year to marry that . . . Ursula!'

I protest: 'He had two children, and there was a war on. He wanted to give us a mother.'

'Give you a mother!' she rants. 'What cheek! What would you have needed a mother for? The Reich would have looked after you. The Reich would have looked after my children, better than any stepmother.'

I say nothing.

Fortunately the Reich collapsed before it could get Peter and me in its clutches. I still shudder at the thought of our narrow escape.

I murmur, almost to myself, 'I didn't want my stepmother, I wanted my grandmother.'

Now my mother gives me a sad look that seems as though it might be genuine.

'Didn't you like Ursula?' she asks softly.

I hesitate. I'd rather not spend too much time on this subject.

'She didn't treat me very well,' I reply curtly. 'And she didn't love me. She never loved me.'

What could I have said about my second mother? That she was my enemy from the first day that Peter and I went to live with her? That after sending me first to a house of correction and then to Eden boarding school, taking advantage of the fact that my father was far away, she managed to persuade him to shut me up in a boarding school again at the end of the war?

I don't say a word, lost in my memories.

'My poor children . . .' she whines now.

'When you were little I called you *Mausi*,' she recalls for the second time, 'and Peter . . .' She frowns. 'I can't remember.'

She sits there sadly for a few minutes, then goes on:

'But you were lively, a little piece of quicksilver you were. You stroked every dog we met and you were very stubborn. You stole bread from the bakery and you liked to hop on one leg. You were always disobedient, and one day you ended up in the pond.'

I know the story about the pond from the version my grandmother used to tell. But now I have the opportunity to hear my mother's account of it. I'm curious.

'How did that happen?' I ask.

'It was in Köstendorf,' she replies without a moment's hesitation. 'I took you there once to let you get a bit of fresh air. There was nothing to breathe in Berlin but hot dust.'

'Köstendorf in Austria?'

'Yes. That's where my uncle's farm was. And there was a pond covered with the leaves and flowers of water-lilies. You thought it was a field, and went happily walking about on it.'

She chuckles with amusement. I was about to drown and she chuckles with amusement at the memory.

'And where were you?' I ask.

She seems suddenly annoyed, and looks elsewhere.

'I can't remember,' she says evasively.

I want to change the subject, but I can't help myself.

'Why not?' I explode irritably. 'How come you don't remember? Where were you when I fell into the pond?'

She looks at me strangely, then, with a threatening and irritable glint in her eyes, she shrieks in a falsetto, 'I won't let you interrogate me! I won't let you!'

But I remember my grandmother's story very clearly.

* * *

With the annexation of Austria, Adolf Eichmann had been sent to Vienna to organise the forced emigration of the Jews, and had set up his general headquarters in the Rothschilds' castle.

The Austrian Jews were summoned to see him there, after which – officially deprived of their citizenship and of any movable or immovable property, and armed only with papers allowing them to cross the border – they were banished from the country, with instructions to leave as quickly as possible and never to set foot on Austrian soil ever again.

My paternal grandmother, who had always been the only intermediary between me and my past, had referred several times to the fact that my mother had had something to do with Adolf Eichmann, but without providing any more detailed information than that. But she did tell me one thing: that when we were on the Köstendorf estate my mother was summoned to Vienna by Eichmann – I think this must have been immediately before he was recalled to Berlin to run the Central Office of Jewish Affairs.

My mother's departure for the capital meant that someone had to be found to look after me. But the farm was very busy at that time, and none of the farm-workers could guarantee that they would be able to look after me full time. So their thoughts turned to Siegele, the thirteen-year-old girl whose task it was, when the weather was fine, to bring the cows to pasture on a vast cultivated area of grass not far from the farmhouse.

They had fitted me with a kind of harness with reins, telling Siegele not to let me out of her sight for so much as a moment, but at some point she left me on my own, so that she could relieve herself. Next time she looked I wasn't there: I had resolutely walked towards the pond, and in a trice I was in the water. Fortunately it wasn't very deep, and I had stopped where the water was still shallow, so she didn't have much difficulty pulling me out. I developed a sore throat, she was solemnly chastised, and there were no further consequences.

It wasn't my grandmother's fault: every time she wanted to bring up the topic of my mother's negligence, of which she herself had washed her hands, the episode with the pond came up again.

In any case, during the time when we were in Köstendorf my mother was pregnant with Peter. Having answered Eichmann's call so promptly, she couldn't take on any other tasks, regardless of what they were.

I look at my mother with a combination of resignation and resentment. A shame: she's avoided the truth yet again. She is sly, unfair, even hypocritical. But she's still my mother. And this is the last time that I'll see her.

With a shudder I seek her eye, but she's being elusive now. She is contemplating herself, looking inside and seeing only what she wants to see. Good God, I think, what will I be left with after this encounter? What truth has she given me during these past two hours, apart from emphasising the few memories that are still dear to her, and which touch her pride or her vanity? She insists on talking about Hilde, for example, my aunt by marriage. She refuses to remember the pond in Köstendorf, preferring to fan the flames of her ancient rancour towards the woman who had introduced my father to the young and lovely Ursula.

'If she hadn't gone to buy "Lions in the Savannah" that day,' she insists, 'she wouldn't have met Stefan, and she wouldn't have gone on to hand him her little sister on a silver platter.' And once again I don't understand. If she was so fond of her husband, why did she leave him in 1941?

And yet I let her go on talking; I want to take advantage of the opportunity to prepare to leave. For another few minutes the object of her resentment will be Hilde, the same Hilde who took my brother and myself to Hitler's bunker in 1944, along with many other Berlin children, so that we could serve in one of Goebbels's many propaganda campaigns. This one was designed to put about the myth of a human and sympathetic Führer who acted as host to hundreds of children in the big bunker beneath the New Chancellery, to give them medicine, food and comfort.

We went to the bunker. I didn't want to. I didn't want to come out of one refuge to go into another one, however much bigger it was, even if it was absolutely enormous: a kind of citadel holding about six or seven hundred people.

It was early December 1944, before the SS drew up the infamous 'Night and Fog' decree, which focused their attention on the anti-fascists and anti-Nazis in the occupied territories, inflicting the most appalling deaths upon them. Hitler's followers were instructed to kill all prisoners of war without exception, along with all anti-fascists held in prisons and concentration camps. Many were murdered merely for 'defeatism'.

My brother and I, I told her, went to the bunker. One morning a camouflaged, coal-driven bus – a '*Kokskocher*' – showed up. We climbed aboard and set off, across a Berlin that was now nothing but an enormous smoking pyre. A month past my seventh birthday, I sat in amazement and gazed out the window at the scene passing before my eyes.

Ruins, then more ruins, some still ablaze, flames reaching into the sky. Piles of corpses were heaped up on the shattered pavements. There was nothing to be seen anywhere but the most savage destruction.

In Hitler's bunker we were given food and medicine: I don't recall so much as a scrap of comfort. We were immediately examined by doctors, chiefly, I should imagine, to avoid any risk of contagion to the Führer, who was about to come and see us . . . We were dosed with vitamins, and with the hateful cod liver oil; we were tested for tuberculosis, and even put under a quartz lamp to make us look healthy and well: the Führer hated to see pale and undernourished children.

Yes, we met him, the Führer of the Third Reich. He came with his bodyguards and shook hands with the children in the front row, including my brother and myself: a troop of unhappy children, trembling with emotion and exhausted by the war.

I stared at the great Führer, and couldn't believe what I saw. To the undeceived eyes of a child, he was a sick-looking, wrinkled old man. He had a limp, one of his arms looked as though it was made of plaster, and his head trembled slightly. But his gaze was still forceful and intense: I felt as though I were being hypnotised by a snake.

I wasn't aware of any benevolence in his question: 'How do you like it in the bunker?' I couldn't detect any pity or sympathy on his part. No, Adolf Hitler didn't like children, any more than my mother did. Shortly before Germany's defeat he sent hundreds of thousands of boys to certain death. I remember two of those young victims, whom I saw abandoned on the edge of a pile of rubble: their eyes were narrowed to slits, their bodies disfigured. What remained of their grey-blue uniforms was nothing but blood-drenched rags; they still wore their flasks around their waists, along with hand grenades, rifle ammunition and gas masks. It was the day after the surrender.

And my mother? Did she ever, even for a single moment, love her children?

Berlin, 1941. District of Niederschönhausen. It was around six o'clock on a cold autumn afternoon.

My mother looked at me severely. 'You've got to be very strong now,' she said, 'Mama has to go away. Aunt Margarete will soon be coming to get you. You're going to go to your aunt's villa – you like your aunt's villa, don't you? And you'll be with your cousin Eva. Do you promise your mother you'll be a good girl?'

'I don't want to go and stay with cousin Eva,' I whined. 'She's always calling me a stupid cow, and won't let me touch her dolls.'

'Well you're going!' my mother says impatiently. 'And so is your brother. And you're going to be good and not drive your aunt Margarete mad. So no more nonsense!'

She spoke very briskly.

'And don't cry!' she ordered, seeing that my mouth was beginning to crumple. 'You're always the same, always whining!'

She was tense, nervous. She was clearly in a hurry.

Terrified, I tried to obey. I sensed that something serious and irrevocable was taking place. I glanced out of the window. Night was falling, and the blackout would soon have to go up.

I hated those horrible rolls of black cardboard. They had been fitted to all the windows by an old workman with only one eye (a souvenir of the first war, he explained) 'on government instructions'. When my father, who had fought in an anti-aircraft division, returned from the front, he told us that all this business with blackouts was so much nonsense: the Allied bomber squadrons were perfectly able, simply by following their radio instructions from headquarters, to locate their targets even if they were flying blind. But no one dared to say that the blackouts in the city were entirely useless: to voice such an opinion during the war would have been considered an act of defeatism.

My mother gave me a quick peck on the cheek and moved towards the little suitcase that was ready and waiting near the front door. I was overcome by panic.

'Don't go away,' I pleaded.

She turned around and stared at me, exasperated.

'Is that how you keep your promises? You promised to be a good girl, and here you are doing nothing but whine. But it's useless, Helga. I've got to go, don't make things so hard for me.'

I tilted my head, and in a heroic attempt to 'be good', I gritted my teeth so as not to burst into tears.

She put on something light-coloured, I think it was a raincoat, and her long wavy hair fell on either side of her face. When she bent down to give me one last kiss, I instinctively grabbed that hair with both hands. 'Don't go away, *Mutti*, please, don't leave me alone.'

She straightened up abruptly and hissed, 'What are you doing? Pulling your mother's hair? You're still exactly the same as you always were, rebellious and naughty! You deserve to be punished.'

But she didn't punish me. She clutched her suitcase and, turning around, said with one finger raised, 'And when I walk through that door you're not to go wailing and waking up your brother, you understand? You promise?'

So many promises in such a short time . . . I stared at her blankly and shrugged my shoulders.

'That's better.' She turned around. '*So, auf Wiedersehen, meine Kleine.*'

I didn't reply. My mother shut the door behind her. I wasn't to see her again for thirty years.

I stood there as though paralysed for a few minutes. Just my heart was beating loudly. I ran to the room where Peter was sleeping.

He was perfectly peaceful, his angelic little face ringed by the blond curls that I had always envied him.

I stopped for a moment and looked at him, and was seized with boundless sadness: I burst into uncontrollable floods of tears. My violent sobs woke him up: he opened his eyes, and when he realised that I was crying, he started howling at the top of his voice, standing up, gripping the edge of his cot. I hugged him. He was shivering. We held each other in a convulsive embrace for a while, then I got my breath back, extricated myself from him and pulled him out of his cot. He needed to be changed. I tried to carry him to the bathroom, but he vigorously objected: he wanted his mother, she was the only one who ever changed him.

I managed to change Peter, but with considerable difficulty. He had scratched me all over. I got exhausted, snapped at him that he was naughty, and went into the kitchen. I took a chair, put it by the window, lifted the roll of cardboard and peeped out.

Darkness had fallen, the air was damp and pungent. The few cars driving along Nordendstrasse had their headlights covered. All the windows of the buildings opposite were black and blind.

My brother was yelling furiously in the bathroom, calling endlessly for his mother in a voice that was by turns imploring and imperious.

He finally came into the kitchen, his eyes bright with tears and rage. He stared at me uncertainly for a few moments, then he started to kick the dresser, accompanying each blow with a raging cry of '*Mutti!*'. I watched his fury with impotence and frustration.

'Stop it!' I tried to tell him once or twice, but he became even angrier. Leave it. He'll get tired on his own, I thought, and go back to sleep. I couldn't wait.

After a while someone rang at the door. I heard shouts outside. 'What's happening? There's a blackout, why is your window wide open?'

I recognised our neighbour's voice and went and opened the door. She looked at me in confusion.

'What's going on, Helga?'

'My mother's gone,' I replied, starting to cry again.

'What do you mean, she's gone?'

I shrugged my shoulders.

She shook her head in disbelief. She came into the house and immediately closed the window and the blackout.

'What on earth got into you, opening the window like that? Don't you know you could be reported?' she yelled at me. Then she leaned over me: 'Where's your mother, Helga? No lies, now.'

'She went away,' I repeated in dismay.

She was still staring at me, but now her face wore a different, strange expression.

'What did she tell you when she went away?' she asked gently. She was quite young, and her hair was braided around her head.

'She told me to be good. She had a suitcase and she went away. She said that aunt Margarete was going to come and get us.'

'Ah, aunt Margarete . . .' the woman echoed, still with that baffled, intent look on her face. She smiled faintly, as though to reassure me, then picked up my brother, who was by now a little calmer.

A few minutes later aunt Margarete turned up. Our neighbour went over to her, worried and anxious.

'Helga says her mother's gone away. What's going on?'

Aunt Margarete confirmed that this was the case. 'Unfortunately it's true,' she replied curtly. She hurried to pack our things and took us with her to her villa in Tempelhof. Aunt Margarete was rich. Her husband, a count, was away at the war, but the villa, which was frequented by the best of Berlin's high society, lacked nothing: there was always some delicacy on the table, while outside the ordinary people were starving to death. Our cousin Eva called Peter and me 'poor people', and wouldn't let us touch her toys.

After some time, having been informed of our aunt's situation, my grandmother arrived from Poland, and immediately decided to take us away . 'I don't want my grandchildren to grow up here with you,' she told her daughter bluntly. 'You would ruin them, you'd turn them into little snobs with a bad smell under their noses.' Long and bitter discussions followed, but my grandmother won in the end, and set up house with us in the flat in Niederschönhausen.

And there we stayed until, less than a year later, my father got married again, this time to Ursula, the young woman from Berlin. And that was when I first found myself in hell.

There has been a long silence. I am aware once again of the mounting tension as the time approaches to say goodbye. It's inexplicable, incongruous: haven't I managed without my mother for my whole life?

I tear my gaze away from the window, and meet her eyes.

'What are you thinking about?' This time she speaks in the tone of a worried, solicitous mother.

The last two hours have made me suspicious. I have learned how to avoid being wrongfooted as she dodges and dives from one position to another.

'What are you thinking about, *Mausi*?' That nickname from long ago touches a very vulnerable part of my soul, but she goes on. She puts her scrawny index finger to my cheek and asks in an almost caressing voice, 'Come and give your old *Mutti* a kiss.'

My stomach leaps into my throat.

I get up and kiss her.

She seems genuinely moved and wipes away a tear.

'Did your second mother kiss you?' she asks all of a sudden.

'No,' I answer, simply.

'Never?'

I shake my head. 'No, never.'

Now she is growing agitated, almost sobbing. 'You should have stayed with Stefan's mother. Not that she was nice to me, she was a bad mother-in-law. But you might have been better off with her than with that . . . that . . .' She twists her mouth. 'It was all Hilde's fault,' she concludes resentfully.

She gets up and goes over to the window. It's stopped raining, but the sky is still dark.

'Hilde, Hilde!' she explodes, and beats a feeble fist against the glass.

'If only a bomb had fallen on her head!' she groans. 'Then she could never have gone to the gallery and bought "Lions in the Savannah"!'

She sits back down on her armchair, and when she lifts her eyes to me, I see that she is eaten up with malign curiosity.

'What happened to her in the end?' she asks. She really is obsessed with that woman.

'Who?' I ask in turn, to gain some time.

'Hilde. Did she ever get married?' She is very alert now, desperate to know.

'No,' I reply. 'After we were repatriated to Austria,

Hilde followed us, or rather, she followed her sister to settle down somewhere nearby.'

'Did she work?'

'She set up a little farm.'

She explodes with laughter.

'So it's true, then, a bad penny always turns up again!'

I don't tell her that Hilde has been dead for many years now. I don't feel like it.

She thinks for a moment. 'Certainly, she was efficient. That was why she worked with Goebbels. Anyone inefficient wouldn't have lasted two minutes with him. And anyway, he himself was a monster of efficiency. That man was a genius.'

She seems to grow distracted, and glances at her empty glass.

'I want another apple juice,' she announces. 'Call Fräulein Inge.' But I'm not going to have the last few minutes of our conversation wasted like that. I throw her some bait: 'I saw Goebbels once.'

'Really?' she bites straight away. 'When?'

I think. 'It was . . . well, Papa had married . . .'

She cuts in: 'Spare me the details.'

That bizarre jealousy again. After fifty-seven years.

She sulks for a few minutes, before her curiosity overcomes her.

'You really saw him? Where?'

'At the Propaganda Ministry on Wilhelmsplatz. I remember lots of banners flapping about on all the buildings . . .'

'And what else?'

'Hilde took us to his office. It was a big office, filled

with light. He struck me as tall and severe . . .'

'But Goebbels wasn't tall,' she objects.

'Yes, but I was a child and had to raise my eyes to look him in the face. He was serious. He barely glanced at me, and immediately turned to Peter. He reached out a hand as though to stroke him, but Peter turned his face away. Only then did he give a half-smile. And he didn't deign to take a closer look at me until Hilde told him my name was Helga, like his elder daughter.'

My mother quickly runs her tongue over her lips, an automatic reaction that you often see in old people. Every time she does it I can't help feeling a twinge of nausea, of disgust.

'And what happened after that,' she persists. It is as if she is waiting to hear the epilogue to a fairy tale.

'My . . .' I break off. Better not to mention my stepmother again. 'At the end we were given some coupons for extra food rations.'

'And Goebbels didn't say anything else to you?'

'I can't remember. The grown-ups talked. Oh, yes, I remember they called him to the phone, and we left without being able to say goodbye properly.' It's not true. The story about the phone call is pure invention.

'And what about the coupons?'

'Ursula got them from a clerk. A tiny little clerk, I remember. A serious little thing who called Hilde "*Fräulein*" rather deferentially.'

'And what else?'

'That's all. We went away. Hilde stayed because office hours weren't over yet. We got home just in time to run to the shelter. Alarms were going off on the corner of Friedrichsruherstrasse.'

The light in her eyes goes out, and suddenly there's an infinite distance between us once again. It takes as little as that for her to be drawn back into the 'old days'.

She murmurs to herself, 'Goebbels was a genius, but I didn't like him as a man. Hilde on the other hand was wild about him, I've always been convinced that she was secretly in love with him . . .' Another of her obsessions, clearly. Her eye runs over me without seeing me, lost in the past.

Immediately after the war, in Berlin, my brother and I were explicitly forbidden to mention Hitler or Goebbels. 'From now on you have to look ahead,' they said, 'the past is past, and the future begins here.'

But what future? I can still clearly see the Berlin of '45. We children played among the rubble while the adults, utterly exhausted, almost guided by animal instinct, did their best to supply us with our daily needs: a scrap of bread, a ration of milk, a pane of glass for the windows . . . No, during those times the people of Berlin had no eyes for the future, or any room for memories.

So it wasn't until 1949 that I heard my aunt Hilde talk about Goebbels. Had she been in love with him? I couldn't say. Certainly she had sad words to say about him, which betrayed great emotion.

It was Christmas. Papa, Ursula, Peter and I had been repatriated to Austria the previous year – my father was a native of Vienna – and we had settled temporarily in the house of my paternal grandparents in Attersee, in the Salzkammergut. In turn my grandparents had been back from Poland for about a year. Hilde had come from Berlin to celebrate the Christmas holidays with us. She had just buried my beloved *Opa*.

It was Christmas Eve. After dinner, and a few bottles of wine, the conversation had grown animated. Only aunt Hilde seemed to become more serious and melancholy, until she finally found relief by bursting into tears. I was dumbfounded. I remembered her from Berlin as always being stern, self-contained and a little distant.

After that outburst she started to remember the old times, when the defeat of the Nazis was still far off, and she was working beside Goebbels in the building of the Propaganda Ministry.

I listened to her in fascination. In spite of everything, Berlin was still close to my heart. One thing that particularly impressed me about her story was the description of the last occasion when she had seen her boss.

Berlin, 21 April 1945: Goebbels had summoned a little group of his immediate circle to the private projection room in his villa overlooking the Tiergarten. It was here that he used to show – to his selected guests, often including the Führer in person – the anti-Semitic propaganda films that he himself had commissioned from the German film industry, of which he was in charge. That morning, however, the atmosphere seemed empty and icy, the windows had been walled up, weak bulbs cast a pale light, and the deafening clamour of battle penetrated the building from outside.

Goebbels turned up late. He was unrecognisable, unshaven, and seemed downcast. He looked like a ghost. Before feeling seized by anxiety, Hilde felt sorry for him.

As well as issuing the usual instructions for the day, Goebbels started shouting and inveighing against the German people, who had not shown themselves worthy of their Führer. The following day, 22 April, as 'Reichskommissar for the Defence of Berlin', he would threaten with a court martial anyone who dared to raise a white flag.

Hilde never saw him again. A few days later she received news of his suicide. He had taken his wife and children with him. Hilde was very upset, even more upset than she had been about the death of Hitler himself.

I couldn't say what Hilde saw in her former boss. Certainly, on that occasion she didn't have a single critical word to say about him. She only recalled little acts of kindness on his part, at parties, or when one of his clerks had a birthday. But as to the feelings that had driven her, they died when she did.

My mother is pondering something.

'Peter turned his face away,' she repeats, absorbed. 'Who was Peter?'

'Your son,' I tell her once again. Little more than an hour has passed since we spoke of him, but she's already completely repressed him from her memory. She is vague again now, her face misty.

'Which one?' She rummages in her memory and frowns.

'You only have one son.'

'That's true . . .' she admits in a faint voice. But it's

clear that she isn't convinced, that she's fumbling around in shadow.

'Do you ever think of him?' I venture. 'Do you ever think about your son?'

She tilts her head. 'I don't know . . . And he died so long ago.'

But now, once again, her tone is uncertain, almost questioning. Remembering what happened before, I fear her reaction, but I want to bring her to some acceptance of reality. I ignore the nudge with which Eva tries to get me to stop.

'Your son is alive,' I say to her gently, in a persuasive tone, as though talking to a child.

Her face drains of all expression. 'That's not true,' she replies darkly. And the scene, as in my worst predictions, repeats itself. My mother plunges her face into her hands, and starts moaning, 'My son died a long time ago . . . Stop telling me lies . . . Stop frightening me . . .'

She's so old, so frail. Once again, in spite of myself, I soften. I am about to go, and am worried that I won't be able to sever the bond that ties me to her. And to think I've tried to do it thousands of times, in thousands of different ways, even denying my own mother tongue.

Some time after my visit to Vienna in 1971, I met a compatriot of mine in Bologna who, naturally enough, started to talk to me in German. It only took a few phrases for me to realise that I could no longer speak my own language fluently and correctly. I was stunned. It was like discovering that I had painlessly lost a limb. A little like in wartime, when a man will lose a leg and go on running till he falls, unaware until then that anything has happened.

It was only after seeking out and finding, after more than fifty years, my cousin Eva, who speaks no Italian, that I was forced to return to my mother tongue. But it wasn't an easy task: it was like climbing, step by step, on hands and knees, a high, steep staircase.

I look at my mother: she's so distant, so unknown, so incomprehensible, so irritating. So disarming, sometimes.

She raises her head and starts begging me: 'Don't leave me alone, never leave me alone again. You've got to come back. You've got to come back every day. I'm your *Mutti*, and nobody loves me. Nobody ever gives me a kiss. You've given me a kiss and I want you to come back. Because you're my *Mausi*.' And she looks at me with a flash in her eye which, if we were speaking about any other woman, I would happily describe as loving.

'My little *Mausi*,' she repeats, and smiles sweetly, affectionately. But it only lasts a moment. And here she is once again, canny and sly.

'It's a shame you're so old,' she hisses. 'I don't like having an old daughter. It makes me feel decrepit. Thank heavens Peter is dead, I couldn't bear to have two children as old as that!' She sighs. 'But you must come back anyway, old as you are. My companions in here have younger children. What a shame that is.'

Something in me freezes. She has already tormented both me and Eva for quite long enough with all this talk of old age. But that's enough now, I say to myself. She's got to stop.

I'm hurt and crushed. She doesn't deserve a thing,

she's cruel, insensitive and lying. She's just vulgar. I shouldn't have come. I should never have listened to Frau Freihorst.

Why did I hurry to Vienna? Perhaps because in spite of everything I can't bring myself to hate her, this mother who isn't a mother?

Make me hate you, mother!

Make me hate you. That would be the best solution. Say something vile about the Jews who were under your guard in Birkenau, those Jews you used to order about, with the power to determine whether they lived or died. The demon that has possessed me suggests my next move, and it's the right one. I make a point of looking at the clock.

'You're not going already?' she says, taking the bait.

'It'll soon be the end of visiting time.'

'I want you to stay!'

Fine, perfect. I reply with false regret, 'I wish I'd known more about you, but you don't talk much. You don't talk much and when you do you break off half-way through. It isn't nice to visit your own mother and not be able to talk to her.'

She grows agitated, rises to her feet, waves her arms around.

'But I do want to talk!'

'It's getting late . . .'

'If I tell you other things will you stay?' She stares at me with pleading in her eyes.

'Perhaps,' I concede vaguely.

'What do you want to know?'

It will have to come of its own accord.

'About Birkenau?' she suggests. But it's basically the

topic that she finds most attractive. Her career, her faith, her iron convictions . . .

'If you like,' I reply innocently. 'For example . . . yes, I'd like to know what sort of relationship you had with the prisoners on your block.'

She hesitates for just a few seconds. Her face, for one wary moment, becomes icy.

'What relationship would you expect me to have with subjects that our government held to be inferior? Inferior and dangerous, which was why they were locked up in the camps in the first place. No relationship whatsoever except the one you have with a hated enemy.'

That's fine, I say to myself, but it still isn't enough.

'Did you just think that way because they made you?' I suggest. 'Or were you personally convinced that the Jews were inferior creatures?'

She hesitates and looks me in the eye.

'Do you want the truth?'

'Yes.'

For a few moments she remains silent and motionless, then she leans towards me and smiles. '*Mausi* . . .' she murmurs, almost deferentially.

She's too close to me, she's making me feel uneasy. And disgusted, I would have to admit. I can smell her breath, the slightly acid breath of an old woman.

Fortunately she draws back, crosses her hands on her bony knees and says in one breath, 'If you want to know the truth, I hated those Jewish women. They gave me an almost physical feeling of revulsion, it turned my stomach to see all those perverted faces, the faces of an inferior race. And how united they were, how they protected each other! They managed to conceal the sick to make sure they didn't end up with Klahr. Yes, my little *Mausi*, I hated those cursed Jews. A horrible race, believe me. *Pfui.*'

I've got what I wanted. I'm stunned, and perhaps she can read it in my face. She looks at me uncertainly.

'I've been open with you,' she declares, 'you mustn't think ill of me. Hating the Jews was an unavoidable duty for a member of the SS, you understand?' She is trying to explain the inexplicable.

'Does that mean you can hate to order?' I ask with a kind of melancholy irony.

'If you are convinced of the reasons, certainly,' she replies very seriously.

'What reasons?'

'The reasons why the Jewish people had to be liquidated.'

I don't take it any further. Instead I ask, 'Why were the prisoners afraid of ending up with that . . . Klahr, you said?'

Even more bitterly than before, she says, 'Yes, I said Klahr. Oh, everyone was afraid of Klahr, they were terrified of him.'

'Who was he?'

'A medical worker. Let's say . . . a sort of specialist nurse.'

'And why were they afraid of him?'

'He was the one that gave the injections.'

'What injections?'

She makes a sharp, decisive gesture, as though stabbing someone in the middle of the chest.

'What does that mean?'

She takes a breath and replies indifferently, 'If a prisoner ended up in the sick bay, the medical wing or the hospital block, and contracted a serious illness, they wasted no time.'

'So what did they do? Tell me!'

'The patient was given an injection.'

'What sort of injection?'

'An injection of phenic acid right into the heart. Zap!' And she repeats the horrible gesture. 'Do you know what phenic acid is?'

I do know what phenic acid is. Not precisely, but I know. Before I have time to compose myself, however, Fräulein Inge comes back in.

'Nearly lunchtime,' she reminds my mother gently. But my mother shrieks, 'I'm not eating today!'

Fräulein Inge nods indulgently. 'Well, we'll see.'

'How much time do we have left?' I ask.

'There'll be another half an hour before all the guests have taken their places and the soup has arrived,' she replies politely. 'I'll come and get your mother at the last minute.'

'I'm not coming!' she shrieks again.

'I know,' Fräulein Inge answers, giving me a little wink. I admire her patience.

So I've got another half hour. I look at her. I'm convinced that she'll have forgotten me soon, perhaps even by this evening, just as she must have done in 1971. And I've done everything I can to remove her from my thoughts.

What a sad couple we are, mother, and what an absurd

bond connects us. We will be the end of each other.

'Will you stay another little while?' she asks, with a tear in the corner of her right eye. Sometimes her voice is so sad and soft.

'Yes,' I reply.

'I don't want to eat,' she repeats. 'I want you to stay with me. Will you stay for a long time?'

'I'll stay for . . . a while,' I answer vaguely.

'Another two hours,' she wheedles. 'And will you call me *Mutti* again?'

Eva nods to me to keep her happy. I'm worn out, and repelled. I say it.

'*Mutti.*'

But the word finds no echo inside me . . .

But she flies off into a great emotional performance. She explodes into a flurry of sobs, blowing me tearful kisses on her fingertips. Until all of a sudden she gets to her feet, comes over to me and kisses me on the forehead.

'Thank you . . .' she says in a broken voice.

She goes back to her armchair, smooths her skirt over her thighs and calms down. Her eyes grow gradually distant again.

I'm bewildered: this new, sudden distance between us worries me. I try to bring her back to me.

'Let's talk a little bit about you,' I suggest once again. 'How do you spend your days?'

But my attempt is unsuccessful. Gesturing impatiently, she snaps, 'I'm going to wait until the evening.'

'But Frau Freihorst often comes to keep you company, doesn't she?'

'Gisela?' she says in a voice that barely conceals contempt. 'She only comes because she gets bored at home without me.'

To me, as to Fräulein Inge before, she denies her friend, her only friend.

'I'm bored here too,' she adds. 'When I was young, life was more exciting.'

She purses her lips, lost in her memories.

'At first things with Stefan were lovely. In Poland we used to ride on horseback and he painted sunsets.'

Her expression becomes bitter.

'But then he changed . . . His mother hated me. And so did his father. My father-in-law was even worse than my mother-in-law, he used to insult me . . . He called me "*Naziweib*", the Nazi woman . . . My mother-in-law wasn't too much trouble at first, but then I had my daughter and she became unbearable . . .'

For a moment she seems to have come to a halt, but then off she goes again. 'In Birkenau, on the other hand, time passed quickly. I had plenty to do, yes, plenty. But of course I had free time as well. And I used it to go and see the work at the goldsmiths' where the prisoners worked. It was very interesting. I had them make me a necklace with letters on it.'

The goldsmiths'. The Jews' gold. Including the gold from the Jews' teeth.

'Don't you want to know what I had them inscribe on it?' my mother asks. I nod weakly.

'*Heidkempe*,' she answers dryly.

'*Heid . . . kempe*? What does that mean?'

'Can't you guess?'

'No. I haven't the faintest idea.'

'It starts with *He*, you see? Helga. And it goes on with the initials of Ida, Krista, Emilie . . . and it finishes with *Pe* . . .'

She comes to a halt again.

'Peter?' I suggest.

Her face clouds over. 'Who is that?'

'Your son,' I reply, exhausted.

'My . . .' She runs her hand over her forehead. 'Yes.' And then she's off again: 'But he died a long time ago.'

She is pensive for a moment, then she goes on.

'One *Lagerführer* got them to make him a Viking ship entirely of gold,' she says. 'It must have been over a foot high.'

She laughs briefly. 'It was a present, you know? A present for his son's fifth birthday.'

She continues unimpeded, articulating her memories. When she wants to remember something, she remembers it very clearly. Her memory is extraordinarily selective.

'A friend of mine in the camp had them make her a gold frame, she was going to put a photograph of her parents in it,' she goes on, 'but it was poisoned. It was poisoned by two female Jewish prisoners. By two filthy Jewish scum. They were taking revenge for something or other, the whores. But of course they were found out, and they ended up in front of a firing squad. Naked. But first they had to spend a fortnight in the punishment block. They were in the dark with rats as big as cats that practically ate them alive. When they got out they were mad with terror, and couldn't wait to get that bullet in the back of the neck.'

She has been speaking through clenched teeth, with

hatred that still seethes inside her like glowing lava.

I feel appallingly torn. Part of me is paralysed with horror; the other, as though acting under hypnosis, goes on asking, wants to know.

'You said *Heidkempe* . . . what were the names in the middle? There was Ida, Krista and . . .'

'Emilie,' she clearly replies.

'Who were they?'

'My sisters.'

My aunts, then. I should have been able to know them, just as I knew my maternal grandparents. How much you have denied me, mother.

'But they've passed on too,' she announces without nostalgia. 'I have no one now. Just the inmates of this barracks. Yes, it is a barracks. They're all unbearable here, including Fräulein Inge. I hate her. And I'm very alone and I have no friends. I have no one now.'

'You've got your friend Gisela,' I try to remind her again.

'Gisela?' My mother denies her for the third time. 'She doesn't count.'

A thought flashes through my head. That something of this woman lives within me, in my genes. I'm repelled, disgusted, but she's already clamouring for my attention again. Her memories are pressing upon her.

'Listen to this! Do you know who I ran into at the camp one day? The wife of a textile trader who had a shop in Niederschönhausen. You remember those big windows full of rolls of fabric?'

No, I really don't remember. I shake my head.

'His name was Guldenmann,' she recalls, 'and his wife was called Emma. They were sent to the camp. He was sent to an *Aussenlager*, and she was sent to the camp laundry. The laundry was in my block. And you won't believe this, but at night she didn't sleep a wink, she would snivel on about her three children who had been taken away from her the minute they arrived, to be sent to the bunker.'

'The bunker?'

'That was what they called the gas chamber.' She says it quite naturally.

'Didn't that make any impression on you?' My voice struggles to emerge from my throat.

'What?' She narrows her eyes, and the blue turns almost white.

'That plant . . .'

'No,' she replies calmly, confidently. 'When I decided to take the *Härteausbildung* I knew very well why I was doing it. It was so that I wouldn't allow myself to be moved by the reality of a camp devoted to . . .' She glances at me cautiously. She hasn't uttered the word 'extermination'. Perhaps, I hope against hope, it's out of a strange kind of delicacy, a respect for my feelings. I'm rather surprised. Besides, it's strange that she was so keen to avoid the term. After all, it isn't one that was used by the Nazis themselves.

'I've wondered from time to time . . .' I murmur.

'What?' she asks, concerned.

I say to myself: get it over with, we'll soon be saying goodbye to each other.

'What have you wondered?' she insists. She pulls herself up in her armchair, and assumes that special interested and open expression that I have learned to distrust.

'I wondered . . . How long . . . how long did it take for the victims of the gas chambers . . .' I can't go on.

'The gas took between three and fifteen minutes to have its effect,' she replies in a detached and technical tone.

'And is it true that after a certain point the exposure time was shortened?'

'Is it that important?' she says, suddenly suspicious.

'Yes, I'd like to know.'

She shrugs her shoulders and her expression becomes opaque. 'I wouldn't know,' she replies evasively.

'You don't know or you don't want to answer?'

She sighs. 'Anyway, that measure became more or less essential.'

'So it was shortened?'

'What was?'

'The exposure time to the gas?'

'Well, they had to get through twelve thousand *Stück* a day; they'd raised the quota.'

I'm struck dumb.

'What are you thinking?' she wants to know.

I shake my head, unwilling to speak.

'What are you thinking?' she insists, running her tongue over her lips once again in that gesture that is so natural and yet so repellent.

I say, 'So it was possible that when you opened the doors of the gas chambers, there might have been some people who weren't quite dead?'

She stiffens, her eyes inscrutable again. 'What on earth are you thinking about?'

'Tell me if you feel like it,' I say, pressing her. My voice is hoarse all of a sudden.

'I don't know.'

I get up. So does she. 'What are you doing? I'm not going to eat,' she whines.

'We read the visiting hours in the hallway,' I hint. 'They'll soon be over.'

She sighs. Now her face is tense and anxious, constantly changing expression.

'Yes, that could happen,' she announces through pursed lips.

'You mean some people mightn't have been dead?'

'Of course!' she cuts in impatiently 'It often happened with children. Sometimes those little *Miststücke* were more resistant to the rat poison than the adults were,' she adds with a sarcastic chuckle. I take my eye off that mocking grimace, and cast a glance at my cousin. She doesn't return it.

There's a pause, but I now know I won't be able to stop. I become aware of a kind of fever welling up in me, an intense craving that won't leave me in peace.

'So the ones that hadn't died ended up along with the corpses in the crematorium, children included?' My forehead is beaded with sweat.

Her face turns frosty and distant.

'I don't know . . .' she replies, hostility in her voice.

'What do you mean, you don't know?' I exclaim aggressively. 'I thought you were seen as a figure of authority at the camp! I thought they always kept you informed about everything that went on.'

My ploy is successful.

'Everyone respected me,' she replies. 'I was an important person!'

'So you were kept informed about the running of the camp?'

'Yes.' She reconsiders: 'Fairly well.'

'And yet you didn't know that people who weren't yet dead sometimes ended up in the crematorium?'

She narrows her eyes and stares into the void. The void is her past. It's all that she has now, towards the end of her days. It's all she has, she hasn't built herself anything else.

At that moment she looks extremely old, quite worn out. She looks at me, and asks desolately, 'What do you want from me? I'm so tired.'

I won't give in. And I reply harshly, 'So you won't give me an answer?'

'To what?' she groans.

'Whether anyone who was still alive ended up with the rest of the corpses in the . . .'

'In the *Krema*?'

'*Krema*?'

'That was what we called the crematorium,' she explains.

She thinks, she stares, she takes a deep breath as though preparing to dive under water.

'Yes, that could happen,' she finally replies with a sigh of resignation. And she continues with the air of someone speaking just because she has a gun pressed to her temple.

'Anyway, not everyone died at the same rate, some people are more resistant to gas than others. And then age was a factor too, as you might imagine? Newborn babies took only a few minutes; they pulled out some that were literally electric blue . . .'

She draws to a halt, because her jaw has begun to tremble again. Her face darkens; she puts an unsteady hand to her jaw to stop it from shaking, to prevent the mournful clicking of her teeth. It's a painful spectacle.

I get up and walk around a little. First I go over to the television, then to an ornamental plant. Mechanically I stroke a stiff, shiny leaf.

'You are evil!' my mother shouts from her armchair, and bursts into violent and convulsive tears. I'm exhausted. I anxiously consult the clock. She doesn't seem able to bear that gesture. 'And stop looking at that clock all the time,' she shrills, 'I don't want you to leave!'

She goes on weeping, although more gently now. I don't know what to say to her. To return to our earlier subject is out of the question. I don't want to say anything at all. I feel drained.

The last thing I expect is the question that she now asks me point blank: 'Didn't you have a son?'

It comes out of the blue. 'Do you remember him?'

'Vaguely . . . He was small.'

'Yes, I brought him to you when I came to get you here in Vienna, in '71.'

'You, in Vienna? With your son? When?'

'Twenty-seven years ago.'

'Twenty-seven,' she repeats. 'Has so much time passed?'

'So much time,' I reply bitterly.

'So when did you come back?'

'We never came back.'

She shakes her head. 'They didn't come back. They didn't come back . . . Never?'

'No, never.'

'But I'm a mother,' she announces suddenly, her voice filled with reproach.

And I'm a daughter, I want to say, rubbing it in. But I say nothing.

There's a pause, and she stares at an empty point in the air.

'Why didn't you come with your child today?' she asks finally, in a disappointed voice.

'He couldn't come for work reasons,' I reply. 'He's a man now. He's thirty-two.'

'Thirty-two? So big already?' She looks astonished.

I nod. 'Yes. Time flies.' I realise I've used an empty cliché, absurd in the context; my mind is enfeebled.

'And is he married?'

'Not yet.'

'And have you a husband?'

'I'm a widow.'

She thinks for a moment. 'He was probably very old,' she calculates.

'My husband died at the age of forty-seven,' I reply.

'Really?' she says in disbelief. She presses two fingers to her temples and emits a deep sigh, as though these revelations were oppressing her mind.

'And have you got enough money?' she finally asks.

I nod. And I think about the gold she wanted to give me in 1971. 'It might come in useful in an emergency,' she had said. And then she had lost me.

'Does he talk about me, ever?' Her face is strained. 'Does my grandson remember me?'

No, she doesn't realise. She can't imagine the trauma Renzo suffered that day in Vienna. He was five years old.

My mother's indifference was a terrible disappointment to him. He had imagined he was going to find a grandmother – because his paternal grandmother clearly preferred her Italian grandsons to one who was half-Austrian – and instead he had found himself being ignored, if not rejected. I had never mentioned my mother to him again.

'Will you bring him one day?' she asks now in a tender voice, with almost convincing emotion.

'Yes,' I lie.

'And will you bring me yellow roses?'

Who knows where this passion for yellow roses comes from. Were they a regular gift from her mysterious boyfriend in Berlin? And what role did he play in her life?

Following the course of these thoughts I must have given an involuntary nod of assent, because my mother goes on, 'And will your son call me *Oma*?'

Oma. Grandma, granny. No, I don't think my son would ever call her that. I look out of the window. The sky is still leaden, and a light rain has started to fall again.

Behind me her voice repeats: 'And will your son call me *Oma*?'

I turn around. I stare into those blue eyes that my son has inherited.

'Yes, he'll call you *Oma* . . .'

At that moment the second gong for lunch rings out. My mother gives a start. 'I don't want to eat!' she shouts, dismayed. 'I want to go on talking to you.'

Her eyes are narrowed, her expression imploring, but her jaw is no longer trembling.

She rises to her feet and takes a few steps towards me. 'Don't go, don't go!'

She grips my arms, she lets herself go, as though she's about to fall on her knees at my feet. I hold her up, and bring her slowly back to her armchair.

'Do you want me to tell you something else?' She knows it's the only way of keeping me there.

I'm standing up, and she has to tilt her head back to look me in the face. In that pose, with her body twisted, her arms folded over her chest, she looks even frailer than before. But there is already a fresh gleam in her eye.

'Do you want me to tell you about the fourth one?'

'The fourth one?' I repeat automatically. I'm in a trap, once again.

My mother composes herself, smooths her woollen military suit over her knee; she casts me a vaguely cheerful glance.

'Well?' I ask brusquely. 'What is this mysterious fourth one?'

'If I tell you, will you stay with me a bit longer?'

I nod.

'A long time?'

'Until Fräulein Inge sends us away.'

'Don't worry, she won't.' She looks confident.

'Well?' I say.

'The fourth crematorium in Birkenau had no ovens,' she begins as though savouring every word, apparently satisfied at having drawn me into her net, 'because it was never finished. All it had was a big well filled with hot embers.'

She leans towards me confidentially: 'The new commander in Auschwitz found it terribly amusing. He used to line the prisoners up on the edge of the well and then have them shot, to enjoy the scene as they fell in.'

I don't want to believe it, I want to be able to think that this story has been invented just to keep me here. But I know she's telling the truth.

A truth that gushes from her lips while she shows not the slightest emotion.

'There was another one,' she continues, 'who amused himself in the same way, but he had Jewish women brought to the well. Naked Jewish women.'

'Who was he?'

'Moll, the man in charge of the crematoria. When he saw them fall into the embers he laughed like a madman. He didn't hate anyone as much as he hated those women, not even the Russian prisoners.'

I free myself from her net. 'But what did you all have against the Jews?'

'Meaning who exactly?' she protests.

'Well . . .' I shrug. 'All of you, Hitler, Himmler, the regime, the SS . . . *You*.'

'They were guilty,' she replies resolutely.

'Of what?'

'Of everything. Of Germany's defeat in the First World War, of constant defeatism towards Germany, of international conspiracies to unleash fresh conflict . . .' She's speaking with absolute conviction, but it's as though she were reciting an old lesson, a well-established litany.

'Stop it,' I interrupt her. I can't take any more. She catches her breath, and in a calmer voice I add, 'It hurts me to know that my mother lived alongside sadists and criminals.'

'Sadists and criminals,' she repeats, struck. 'It's very hard to hear your daughter say that.'

'I know,' I answer dryly.

She falls silent, and seems to reflect for a moment. 'Perhaps you're right,' she says, 'even if you're only partly right. War changes people, and it changed many of us as well.'

So she's justified, exonerated. It's unbearable.

'War has nothing to do with extermination!' I explode. 'Gas chambers aren't war! Ovens in crematoria aren't war!'

'I didn't come up with the Final Solution,' she replies, on the defensive, 'I was only obeying orders. I had to stay loyal to my oath, and an oath is sacred. And I'll tell you something else, and it doesn't matter whether you believe me or whether you don't. Among my comrades in the SS I knew people who were intelligent, cultured, responsible, excellent family men like Rudolf Höss . . . Men of honour, unforgettable men . . .'

Men of honour . . . lovers of nature, of hearth and home, of animals . . . The stock Nazi self-portrait, kitsch at its most loathsome.

I look at Eva. She is very pale. I try to stay calm. I scour my mind for the least aggressive reply. 'Excuse me,' I say unemphatically, 'but calling the SS "men of honour" frankly seems excessive to me.'

My mother's reaction is sudden and sharp: 'If you say that about the men, then that means there were no women of honour. And what would that make me? Do you really see me as a criminal, as the military tribunal did? Is that how you see your mother, tell me now? It's about time we started saying what we meant!'

She's beside herself.

I wait a few seconds before replying, and try not to raise my voice: 'How do you think I see a mother who was a guard at Birkenau?'

She doesn't hesitate for a moment. 'Well, my daughter, like it or not, I have never regretted being a member of the Waffen-SS, is that clear?'

Oh, that's clear, mother, I never doubted it for a moment.

'And you should know this, too,' she goes on proudly, 'that I was the one who put myself forward to be assigned to one of those camps – and do you want to know why? Because I believed in it. I believed in Germany's mission: to free Europe from that . . . from that repugnant race.'

Get up, go: that should be my reply. And instead I ask once again, as I did before, 'Didn't you even feel sorry for mothers with newborn babies at their breasts when they went into the gas chambers? Didn't you even feel sorry for the children?'

I should have understood that there was nothing left to say. So what do I want? Why am I asking the same questions over and over again?

She looks uncertain for a moment. She fixes her eyes in the distance. Her breathing becomes irregular, as though she's climbing a steep flight of stairs. Then all of a sudden she calms down, raises her eyes, stares at me. Everything in her has changed: her expression, her gaze, her voice. Everything is new to me.

'All right,' she says slowly. 'Now tell me the answer you want me to give.'

She has wrongfooted me again. 'I don't understand.'

She has a strange look in her eye.

'Didn't you ask me a question? Well, tell me what answer you want me to give.' She is more calm and lucid than I have ever seen her before. There's a mocking note in her voice, mixed with a kind of almost affectionate condescension.

I'm really confused. I have a sense that all of a sudden, thanks to some trick that she has slipped past me, she has assumed the upper hand.

'So?' she says, pressing me in that same slightly mocking tone. 'Don't you know what to say? Don't you know what answer you want me to give to your nasty, wicked, malicious question?'

She assumes an indulgent air and shakes her head. 'My poor *Mausi*, I've left you speechless.'

Is it possible that at the very last minute she's going to grant me a hint of benevolence, a scrap of warmth?

My head is spinning slightly, I'm not even sure that I can remember my 'nasty, wicked, malicious question'. Nonetheless I reply like an automaton: 'I want you to answer sincerely, that's all.'

To hell with the question. I'm exhausted. I wish I were back in my taxi already, on my way back to the hotel, and then going to dinner with Eva in a restaurant in the city centre. I have a craving for Viennese cooking, for dark beer.

'Fine,' says my mother. 'So you want the truth, unadorned. Are you sure?'

'Yes.'

She joins her hands together, takes a deep breath, and relaxes the furrows on her broad, white brow.

'I'd really rather be able to tell you something else, but since it's the truth you're after . . . Well, then you shall have it.'

All of a sudden I feel an impulse to bring everything to a halt, to ask her to be quiet, to go. But I suppress it.

'As far as I was concerned, what was right for the government was right for me,' she begins in a firm voice, 'and I had no right to any kind of personal thoughts, opinions or feelings. Rather I had the duty to obey, without argument, orders from above, and if those orders meant the gassing of millions of Jews then I was willing to collaborate. Which is why, believe me, I could not allow myself even the slightest weakness over mothers or children. When I saw the littlest ones going into the bunker, all I could think was: there's a few less Jewish brats, there are some kids who will never become repellent adult Jews.'

She comes to a halt, battles against the incipient tremor in her jaw, then decides to ignore it and continues. At that moment she is very strong.

She looks at me, clearly and directly. 'I was convinced of the rightness of the Final Solution, and so I carried out my tasks with great commitment and conviction. Consequently I was treated as a criminal, but even during my detention I never stopped feeling proud, and worthy, to have belonged to the Germany of our great Führer . . . Did you know I read Kant in Birkenau?'

Her eyes gleam. She's going to take her errors with her to the grave, I think with a shudder.

'The world didn't understand,' she adds, her voice still hoarse with grievance, 'and in the end they all joined forces to destroy us.'

She looks at me with an expression of apparently genuine regret.

'If you hoped I was going to change my mind, I'm sorry to have to disappoint you. I'm staying the way I was.'

And she concludes, 'I've told the truth, the whole truth. The truth you wanted.'

The truth I wanted . . .

A dense silence has fallen in the room. My mother seems lost in that far-off other place. Has she been truly sincere, or has she said what she thought I wanted to hear – something that would help me to hate her definitively, to free myself from her once and for all?

She lifts her head and studies me through half-closed eyes, as though trying to bring me into focus. A twisted, ambiguous smile plays on her lips. It only lasts a moment, then she turns towards the window and starts playing with the hem of her jacket. The movements gradually become slow and mechanical, until she is motionless, with a piece of material wrapped around a finger. She has slipped away. And I realise that if, until yesterday, her absence was a presence that obsessed me, now her presence is an irrevocable absence. I feel anxiety and an irrational tenderness. She is my mother; in spite of it all she's my mother. Should I be ashamed if, every now and again, instinct, my instinct as a daughter, gets the better of morality, of history, of justice and humanity?

Eva brushes my arm: she gives me a sympathetic smile. She nods helplessly towards my mother. I understand that she shares my feelings. A moment later Fräulein Inge comes back in.

'They're waiting for you in the dining room,' she tells my mother in a briskly professional voice. 'Shall we go?'

My mother seems to be waking from a brief sleep.

'I'm not coming!' she announces, immediately becoming noisy and belligerent. 'I'm not eating today. I have to talk to my daughter again.'

'Visiting hours are over,' Fräulein Inge insists, 'and it's time for you to come to lunch.'

'I said I wasn't going to!'

My mother gets to her feet, her face contorted. 'You go to lunch if you're so fond of it, and leave me alone with my daughter!'

'I really think it's time for you to say goodbye to your guests,' Fräulein Inge replies very firmly. 'Give me your hand like a good girl.'

But my mother yells, 'I just want my daughter's hand! I don't want anyone else's hand!' And with a swift, unruly gesture she hides her left hand in her armpit, like a stubborn, capricious child.

Fräulein Inge gently detaches that rebellious hand and grips it in her own. My mother yells furiously, 'She's hurting me! Help, she's hurting me!'

She struggles and manages to break away, then dashes towards me. 'You hold me. You hold me!' she begs, gripping my hand. And she smiles trustingly.

I feel a mixture of embarrassment and pain – and an instinctive sense of protectiveness.

'Don't go . . .' she pleads, 'don't go . . .' And her cold and bony fingers spasmodically clutch at my own.

'I'm alone, no one ever comes to see me here . . .' she stammers.

Once again Fräulein Inge reminds her: 'Doesn't Frau Freihorst come three times a week to keep you company?'

My mother pushes out her lower lip: 'I don't care, I just want my daughter.'

Fräulein Inge shakes her head and says nothing. She gestures to me to leave the room with my mother. I obey, tired and confused.

The corridor is filled with the usual lunchtime sounds: a rattle of plates, a hubbub of voices, the service staff pushing trolleys full of glasses, cutlery and food.

Fräulein Inge walks ahead of us towards the door of the dining room. We're about to walk in when all of a sudden my mother wrests her hand from mine, and, making a sudden lunge, hurls her arms around my neck.

'Don't leave me,' she sobs, 'don't go!'

Silence falls all around. The only sound is my mother weeping beneath the vaults. Everyone is looking at us in consternation.

Now my mother presses her head against my chest and groans, 'Stay with me. Stay with me . . .'

Fräulein Inge tries to free me from the grip of those frail and scrawny arms which reveal, in that wild embrace, an unexpected strength. My mother's sobs are becoming louder and louder, she struggles, then all of a sudden she starts kissing me everywhere: she kisses the sleeves of my jacket, my buttons, my pearls, my lapel with the brooch I bought in Venice one foggy day.

She kisses the palms of my hands . . . it's terrible.

It's as though a veil were being torn. Now the whole of our story is here. The failed story of a mother and a daughter. A non-story.

Let me go, mother.

Finally Fräulein Inge manages to separate us. She puts her hands sympathetically on my mother's shoulders.

'Now you have to be sensible and say goodbye to your guests.

Eva whispers to me, 'Tell her we'll be back in the afternoon.'

I comply: 'Now you go to lunch, and I'll be back in the afternoon.'

In my mother's eyes, still wet with tears, there is a flash of joy. 'Are you serious?'

'Yes.'

'You promise?'

'Yes.' I'm ashamed.

Then my mother frees herself with an irritated jerk from the hands of Fräulein Inge, and solemnly announces, 'I'm going to eat because my daughter has promised she'll be back in the afternoon. And I believe my daughter because she is a woman of her word. My daughter doesn't tell lies. My daughter isn't one of those people who promise to do something and then don't do it. She is sincere. She is my daughter, and I believe her.'

For another few minutes she studies me with painful intensity and then, with a gentleness of which I wouldn't have thought her capable, she asks, 'Will you give me another kiss, *Mausi*?'

I feel a sharp pain in my heart, searing as a wound.

And I kiss her. I lean forward and kiss my mother's icy cheek. The more I lean over, the more she seems to shrink. I want to call her *Mutti*, but the word stays imprisoned in the pit of my stomach. I search for an affectionate gesture; I clumsily clasp one of her shoulders. I may have hurt her, but she smiles contentedly.

A relentless feeling of unreality. Once again I wonder who it is that I'm looking at.

Were you really an inflexible Nazi, mother, or did you say all those horrendous things to help me to hate you?

I look at her trusting eyes, reflected in mine, and think: no, I don't hate her. It's just that I don't love her.

'It's time to go,' Fräulein Inge repeats, calmly but firmly.

My mother meekly obeys.

'See you later,' she smiles. 'See you later, my daughter.' And she sets off towards the dining room, towards the hubbub of voices. I watch her as she goes. At the last moment, before passing through the doorway, she turns around and blows me a kiss on her fingertips. Once again she has a strange expression on her face. And once again I feel that she is irrevocably remote from me.

I lose myself in my thoughts, and when I re-emerge my mother isn't there. I have a cold, empty feeling. I stare at the double door of the dining room, perhaps I make as though to head in that direction, because Eva holds me back by one arm.

'We've got to go . . .' she whispers to me.

I nod, and think: I've lost.

I've lost again.

'If you like we can speak on the phone,' Fräulein Inge suggests.

I gratefully accept, and she hands me a piece of paper with her home phone number.

'You can even call late in the evening,' she says amicably.

'I'll call you from the hotel,' I reply, touched.

'She's in good hands,' she assures me with a smile of farewell.

My cousin leads me arm in arm along the corridor, towards the stairs. My throat is tight, I can barely breathe.

'It's over,' Eva whispers affectionately. And I let myself go and start crying.

At the porter's lodge we ask them to call us a taxi. I am unsteady on my feet. There's that violent sense of unreality again. What has happened?

What has happened?

I raise my face, the mild rain refreshes my forehead.

'It's over,' my cousin repeats. 'It's all over, relax.'

An iron sky lies heavy over the tops of the old plane trees, the air is damp and clammy.

The taxi stops outside the gate.

Before getting in, Eva turns and asks me, 'Do you think you'll be coming back?'

PUBLISHER'S NOTE

Helga Schneider's mother was sentenced by
an Allied jury to serve a six-year prison term for minor
war crimes and for having been a member of the SS.
Since she cooperated fully with the investigating
commission, she ultimately served a reduced sentence.
Dossiers that document her work as an SS guard are on
file in various archives, including the Wiesenthal Center
in Vienna and Auschwitz.

The visit chronicled in this book took place in 1998.
It was the last time Helga Schneider would see her
mother, who died in 2001.